The Ascendant

by

Jodie Forrest

Published by Seven Paws Press

POB 2345, Chapel Hill NC 27515
Tel. 919.929.4287; fax 919.929.7092

info@sevenpawspress.com
www.sevenpawspress.com

ISBN: 978-0-9790677-0-9
Library of Congress Control Number: 2007900025

First Edition
First Printing, January 2007

Cover concept: Jodie Forrest
Cover photos: Steven Forrest

For information and orders of additional copies, please contact Seven Paws Press.

The soul does not like to be without its body, because without the body it cannot feel or do anything; therefore build a figure in such a way that its pose tells us what is in the soul of it.

—Leonardo da Vinci

Clothes make the man. Naked people have little or no influence upon society.

—Mark Twain

There will be time, there will be time
To prepare a face to meet the faces that you meet;
There will be time to murder and create,
And time for all the works and days of hands
That lift and drop a question on your plate.

—T.S. Eliot

ACKNOWLEDGMENTS

Thanks to:

Scott Ainslie, Joyce Allen, Lynn Bell, Matt Bennett, Renee Bergner, Maryska Bigos, the entire Blue Sky Ranch Fellowship, Jim Bowe, Shalini Chatterjee, Clouseau the Cat, Cynthia Cole, Don Comer, John and Barbara Conner, Paul Cory, Carol and Mike Czeczot, Jim Dennis, Mitch Easter, Leela and Jim Ellis, Jim Fabish, Kelli and David Fox, Tracy Gaudet, Wells Gordon, Jeff and Martina Green, Mary Green, Nicholas Grier, Robert and Diana Griffin, Dave and Donna Gulick, Jeff Hamilton, Kathryn and Scott Hammond, Laura Haywood-Cory, Ellen Hemphill, Felicia Herman, Jeff Jawer, Rhiannon Jones, Tim Lajoie, Alphee and Carol Lavoie, Rob Lehmann, Catherine Losano, Michael Lutin, Manda the Cat, The Mountain Astrologer; Laura, Maggie and Greg Nalbandian; Vinessa Nevala, Debby Ostlund, Andre Pelliciari, Starr and Mike Perry, Piedmont Karma Thegsum Choling, Lina Pratt, the late Pyanfar the Cat, Melanie Reinhart, Keith Rhyne, Paul Richard, Evelyn Roberts, Pauline Rodick, Dag and Sharon Rossman, Jim Roy, Savannah Scarborough, Philip Sedgwick, Steve Sky, Cristina Smith, Tom Stevenson, Joey Swails, Diane Swan, Brian Trent, Shelley Wawrzonek, Muriel Williman, Harriet Winokur, Sanford Wolcott, Scotty Young, and the Zapatistas of the Dead.

Special thanks to:

Ingrid Coffin and Chris Zydel, who coordinate my astrology intensive workshops with infinite sanity, supportiveness, love, patience and humor.

Diana Stone, who graciously allowed me to reference her excellent and insightful material on the Ascendant and her "Communication Model for Astrologers."

My husband, Steven Forrest, for the cover photos, for patiently waiting to be surprised with the text of this book until after its publication, and for twenty-five miraculous years together and counting.

For my students and my clients,

from whom I have learned so much,

and from whom I am still learning.

THE ASCENDANT

Table of Contents

INTRODUCTION

I almost wrote this book about twenty years ago. I've been thinking about it ever since.

Why didn't I write it then? For several reasons.

First and foremost, crafting my own fiction was more compelling. I abandoned a novel in progress to co-author the first version of *Skymates* with my husband, Steven Forrest, for Bantam Books. My historical fantasy novels, the "Rhymer" trilogy beginning with *The Rhymer and the Ravens,* took ten years to write, with a year off between the first and second books to start my own Seven Paws Press in 1995.

Secondly, with me as editor in chief, Seven Paws Press took on its own momentum. After the trilogy, Seven Paws Press published two books by Steven and our friend and colleague Jeffrey Wolf Green: the two volumes of *Measuring the Night*, which I edited into book form from lecture transcripts. Seven Paws Press then published: Steven's mystery novel, *Stalking Anubis*; the revised and expanded edition of Steven's and my co-authored book, *Skymates: Love, Sex and Evolutionary Astrology*; Rafael Nasser's brainchild, *Under One Sky*, in which twelve astrologers, all working blind, analyze the same birth chart; Steven's and my co-authored book, *Skymates II: The Composite Chart*; and Douglas "Dag" Rossman's book, *The Northern Path: Norse Myths and Legends Retold . . . And What They Reveal*. During those publishing projects, Steven and I also co-wrote two computerized astrological synastry reports for AIR Software, and I edited them extensively for Ivillage.

Finally, Seven Paws Press is only part of my work. I manage its website, sevenpawspress.com, which also serves as Steven's and my website. I manage the daily operations of Steven's and my combined businesses, and I see my own astrology clients and students.

I stay busy, but I've never stopped thinking of a book about the Ascendant—the book you now hold in your hands. The time to write it finally arrived.

Time is an important concept when discussing the Ascendant, the exact degree and minute of whichever of the twelve signs was rising at the precise moment of birth.

The Ascendant is the chart configuration that took the longest for me both to understand and to learn to explain to my students and my clients. Why? Perhaps because it took some time to get my own Ascendant working comfortably with my Sun and Moon. And probably because of the nature of the Ascendant itself. It's not nearly so straightforward a concept as the Sun (the ego, the identity) and the Moon (the emotional needs and reactions, the feelings).

The Ascendant itself develops over time. It's partly innate: it's our on-the-surface social self; our mask; our "vibes;" our initial style upon meeting strangers. *But it's also a learned response* to our interactions with our environment, as well as to our own internal dictates. Small children don't yet have their Ascendants in proper working order. That's why they're seldom poised. That's why they blurt out funny, revealing and all too honest comments that can make their parents or teachers writhe with embarrassment. We're not born wearing a functional Ascendant any more than we're born wearing clothes.

Can we change our Ascendants?

"Can the Ascendant adapt?" might be a better question. Here, to my mind, are two even better ones: Can the Ascendant grow? Can it evolve?

Yes, it can. And the Ascendant *should* evolve, in response to the transits, progressions and arcs that involve it. Those changing astrological energies that affect our birth charts indicate what we need to learn in order to keep our surface selves—our Ascendants—working for us, rather than against us.

Yes, the Ascendant can grow and change. Yes, but . . . can we change our bodies? Can we change our skins?

In this book, I discuss these concepts and more:

* the Ascendant defined both literally and metaphorically

* its parallels to psychologist Carl Jung's concept of the persona
* the relationship of the actor's craft to the Ascendant
* the Ascendant and one's "style"
* Sun-Moon-Ascendant interactions
* natal aspects to the Ascendant
* the ruler of the Ascendant
* transits, progressions and arcs involving the Ascendant
* how to "adjust" your Ascendant
* humor, the Ascendant and a country's national character
* the Ascendant, physical appearance and rectification tips
* the Ascendant and evolutionary astrology

Finally, the book concludes with an Ascendant "cookbook," where I'm sure many of you have already turned to read about your own Ascendants and those of people close to you.

Before we begin, here's a note primarily addressed to astrologers who see clients, and to students of astrology who intend to do readings:

You have the privilege and responsibility of being your clients' guide through their birth charts. You may well be the only guide they'll ever have through that intricate, perplexing, dynamic astrological material with its capacity for growth and change. Meanwhile, astrology is a vast, complicated and, for most astrologers, an addictively absorbing subject. The advent of computers has fueled new astrological hypotheses and postulates, many of them fascinating enough to lure the practitioner far from the main roads through a birth chart. My nearly 24 years of astrological practice have taught me that it's all too easy for clients to get lost in those side trips—I lost more than a few people there myself, before I realized I should stay on the main road. Don't get me wrong: astrologers *need* visionaries and experimenters to explore those side alleys—some of them eventually proving to lead somewhere useful, and some of them proving blind—or our craft won't grow. But we also need a thorough grounding in astrological theory and practice (and in basic counseling skills) before we can communicate effectively with our clients, most of whom aren't astrologers and don't know our jargon.

I want to discuss the Ascendant theoretically and speculatively in this book and, I hope, to stimulate your own thinking about the subject. But I also want to maintain a practical thread throughout the text: how astrologers and students of astrology can *use* this material in a comprehensible and helpful way with their clients and friends. To that end, wherever I could, I added some study exercises to help you learn and experiment with these concepts.

It's my hope that by the time you've finished this book, your understanding of the Ascendant, this complex and partially self-created astrological configuration, will be far more than skin deep.

Jodie Forrest
Chapel Hill, NC
Winter Solstice, 2006

CHAPTER ONE: WHAT IS THE ASCENDANT?

The Concrete, "Astronomical" Definition of the Ascendant

This definition's easy, at least at first. Your Ascendant is the degree and minute of the zodiacal sign that was rising in the east at the moment of your birth. That makes your Ascendant the cusp (beginning) of your first house. If you have 3 degrees and 15 minutes of Gemini at the cusp of your first house, we say you have Gemini rising or a Gemini Ascendant.

Now things become more complicated. What if your Ascendant is 3 degrees 15 minutes of Gemini, and your second house begins at 5 degrees Cancer? You still have Gemini rising, even though your first house contains a few of the early degrees of Cancer.

What if you have 3 degrees 15 minutes of Gemini rising, and you have Venus in 10 degrees of Gemini in the first house? In my opinion, while the planet Venus remains the planet Venus in its own right—the part of the psyche that has the most to do with relating and creativity—if your Venus is in your first house, it should also be considered part of your Ascendant. We say you have Gemini rising with a first house Venus in Gemini.

In addition to Venus in Gemini in the first house, suppose you have Mars in the first degree of Cancer, and therefore in the first house? (Remember that the second house in this example begins at 5 degrees Cancer.) Then again, while the planet Mars remains the planet Mars in its own right—your inner warrior and guardian, your will and drive—in your case, your Mars should also be considered part of your Ascendant. We say you have Gemini rising with a first house Venus in Gemini and a first house Mars in Cancer.

To summarize, the Ascendant is the sign that was on the cusp of the first house at the moment of birth, and also any contents of the first house. (Later I'll discuss some techniques for interpreting those first house planets.)

Since birth is a process that can take a long time, a question arises here: what precisely *is* "the moment of birth"? Is it when the baby's head crowns? When the baby takes its first independent breath? When the umbilical cord is cut?

I don't know the answers to those questions. Perhaps there's even a different answer for every baby. If any obstetricians or midwives are reading these pages, they doubtless have better ideas than I do about what constitutes the exact moment of birth, and I'd be glad to hear from them. For the purposes of this book, however, let's keep in mind that the definition of "birth" isn't carved in stone.

Nor is the definition of the Ascendant. Which leads us to . . .

Some Abstract and Metaphorical Definitions of the Ascendant

Imagine that you're at a big splashy party where no one knows anyone else. Imagine, too, that all the guests are in relatively good mental and emotional health. For the first fifteen or twenty minutes of that party, all the first impressions given and taken will relate directly to everyone's Ascendant. Who's gladhanding all the newcomers and working the room? Who's retreated into a corner where she can watch everyone and be seen by as few people as possible? Who's asking the host if he needs any help? Who's commandeered the stereo?

Now imagine that two years have rolled by, and you've become good friends with some people you met at that party. Let's say that your first impressions of Joe from the party are a good match for your knowledge and opinion of him now. In that event, there's probably a lot of harmony between Joe's Ascendant and his Sun and/or Moon. But your view of Mary today is completely different than your first impressions of her from that party. In that case, her Ascendant is probably out of kilter with her Sun and/or Moon. We'll discuss the concept of Sun-Moon-Ascendant blends in Chapter Five.

The Ascendant is like the uniform or the clothing that the chart wears, and also like a costume or a mask. Consider all the purposes of clothing. It covers the body. Depending on its fit, it hides some parts of the body and enhances others. It protects us. It expresses us. It says something about who we are, the mood we're in and the role we're playing that day. Dreams in which we realize that we're naked probably have much to do with some trouble that we had adjusting our Ascendants to the demands of the day before, or with some fear that we'll have such trouble tomorrow.

The Ascendant is like our skin. There's a French phrase for feeling comfortable and centered: *Je suis bien dans ma peau.* Literally, it means "I am well in my skin." Metaphorically, it means "I'm comfortable in my skin; I'm at ease in my skin." Our skin is superficial, in that it's on the surface, but it's also absolutely necessary. How would you like to have your skin peeled away? That's how it feels when your Ascendant isn't functioning. You feel raw, naked and vulnerable. You want to cloak yourself, to hide while you lick your wounds.

Many astrological writers have commented that the Ascendant is like a filter over the rest of the chart. The outside world sees a person through that filter, and the filter colors their perceptions of her. Also, the person sees the outside world through the filter of her Ascendant, and it colors her perceptions of the world. The Ascendant is in charge of our relations to the outside world, and it puts its own spin on those "foreign relations."

Another way to describe the Ascendant is to call it the "mouth" of the chart. If you discovered a new species of animal, you could make some good guesses about its diet by observing its mouth and its teeth. Sharp pointy teeth typically belong to carnivores. Wide flat ones usually belong to herbivores. Similarly, the Ascendant describes the experiential food you need to nourish the rest of your chart, the kind of experiences you need to "eat" throughout your life. I don't recall who first said, "The Sun is who you are, and the Ascendant is the path you need to walk in order to become who you are."

A friend of mine, while talking about her body, once said, "That's just my spaceship; it's not who I really am." I love the spaceship metaphor for the Ascendant. *Like the body, the Ascendant is a vehicle in which we travel through space and time, and through which we experience the world.* In science fiction novels or movies, you can tell something about a race of beings by their spaceships. Are the ships bristling with armaments? Do they have huge windows and tons of observation lounges? Do they fly so erratically that they must obey the laws of some *very* strange, non-human physics? Their spaceship contains those beings, but they are more than their container. Our Ascendants "contain" the rest of our charts, and we experience and navigate the world through our Ascendants.

The Ascendant has parallels with the psychologist Carl Jung's concept of the *persona*. The two concepts, Ascendant and persona, are not identical, but the persona is well worth discussing for the light that it can shed on the Ascendant. We'll explore the concept of the persona in greater detail in Chapter Two. Let's define it briefly here, however, using Jung's own words, from "The Relations between the Ego and the Unconscious," in *Two Essays On Analytical Psychology* (1928; rpt. *Collected Works 7*, Princeton, NJ: Bollingen, 1967):

> The persona is a complicated system of relations between individual consciousness and society, fittingly enough a kind of mask, designed on the one hand to make a definite impression upon others, and, on the other, to conceal the true nature of the individual. That the latter function is superfluous could be maintained only by one who is so identified with his persona that he no longer knows himself; and that the former is unnecessary could only occur to one who is quite unconscious of the true nature of his

> fellows . . . the construction of an artificial personality
> becomes an unavoidable necessity. The demands of
> propriety and good manners are an added inducement
> to assume a becoming mask. What goes on behind the
> mask is then called "private life."

"The construction of an artificial personality" or mask is indeed "an unavoidable necessity" in modern life. Note those words "construction" and "artificial." While we are to some extent born with Ascendants, as we are born with bodies, *the Ascendant, like the persona, is something we construct ourselves, over time, and partially in response to the socialization process.*

Since the era of Jean-Jacques Rousseau's "noble savage," Westerners have been apt to romanticize the "natural" man and woman and, to some extent, to demonize the effects of civilization. Nevertheless, we are social creatures. We do not live in total isolation from one another.

But what if we did? What would our Ascendants be like if we didn't grow up in the midst of human society and have to adapt to its pressures and demands? Would we even *have* Ascendants, in Jung's sense of the persona?

I suspect that we would. The minute you meet a stranger or have to interact with someone you don't know well, such as your bank teller, it's your Ascendant that interacts with him or her. Furthermore, it's hard to imagine a human being who has had absolutely *no* contact with any other people. How could such a child survive? In the adult world, someone without a functional Ascendant makes others uneasy, regardless of whether the Ascendant is damaged because of inadequate socialization or because of mental illness. Such a person is called mad or dangerous or sick, unless that person is a child. Even then, some of the truths children blurt out can make us uneasy.

Since a picture is worth the proverbial thousand words, I started wondering how the arts treated themes related to the Ascendant. In the 1994 feature film *Nell*, Jodie Foster plays the title character, a thirty-something woman who was raised by her hermit mother in the North Carolina mountains. Nell's mother's speech was terribly impaired by a stroke that occurred sometime in Nell's childhood. Other than her mother and a twin sister who died when Nell was a little girl, Nell has never interacted with another human being.

When her mother dies, Nell is found by the doctor (played by Liam Neeson) who signs the death certificate. Nell speaks a strange combination of an invented twin language and all but incomprehensible English, and she's very fearful of leaving her cabin during the day—her mother may have instilled this fear to try to keep her safe. Psychologists are consulted, and want to remove Nell from the cabin and civilize her. Meanwhile, the doctor insists that she's a self-sufficient adult who hasn't asked for help. Gradually he learns Nell's language. Meanwhile, redneck locals with less than admirable values become curious about the "wild woman," and the media picks up her scent.

The movie follows a fairly predictable trajectory, with Nell removed from and then returned to her woodland environment, and her superior "noble savage" wisdom affirmed. It's a silver screen fantasy—and well worth seeing just to observe how Jodie Foster inhabits the body language, movement and affect of an "uncivilized" woman. Foster was nominated for a "best actress" Academy Award for her performance.

I recommend that you rent *Nell* and, when you watch it, that you think about the Ascendant. Nell has developed virtually no persona. She has no way to streamline or summarize or mask herself for others. Therefore, she has very little way to protect her innermost being. With Nell, what you see is what you get. Not just her heart but her entire self is written all over her face. How genuine. How vulnerable. And, without the protective shell of an Ascendant, *how terrified we are about what could happen to Nell out in society.*

Another movie that explores the territory of the Ascendant, but in a totally different way, is Ingmar Bergman's aptly named *Persona*. In this 1966 film, Liv Ullmann plays actress Elisabeth Vogler who, in the middle of a performance, suddenly stops talking. There's no physical reason for her refusal to speak, so her psychiatrist sends her to an isolated summer house under the care of a young nurse (played by Bibi Andersson) named Alma. "Alma" means "soul"—and that double meaning is just one of the many layers of this fascinating and enigmatic film.

Actors need flexible personas, in order to shed them temporarily as they assume their roles, as they step into their characters' skins. (We'll discuss acting and the Ascendant in Chapter Three.) Elisabeth has stopped acting on-stage, has lost both her own persona and that of her character. Her muteness implies that she's no longer acting off-stage either.

Were she not mute, her Ascendant would handle her early interactions with Alma. If we have no persona, does our soul show through? What's the relationship of the persona to the soul? Faced with Elisabeth's silence, Alma, whose name means "soul," begins chattering compulsively.

As the film progresses, Alma's conversation becomes more and more personal, intimate and revealing. One night, while drinking heavily, Alma reveals that she and a woman friend once participated in an orgy on a beach with some teenage boys they didn't know. The sex was surprisingly good; she got pregnant; she had an abortion. She's not sure she really loves her fiancé. Elisabeth's face seems to show that she's listening compassionately, but she says nothing. That night, the film shows her entering Alma's room and leaving again, but she denies it the next day, and both Alma and the film's audience are confused about whether the visit actually happened.

Then Alma reads a letter she's mailing for Elisabeth, who refers to Alma's "infatuation" with her and to the tale of the orgy, and writes that Alma makes "a good study." Enraged and feeling betrayed, Alma starts a series of verbal attacks on Elisabeth, who remains mute until Alma threatens to throw a pan of boiling water in Elisabeth's face (the face is a symbol of the persona). Then Elisabeth says only, "Don't!" Alma claims that Elisabeth doesn't love her son and bore him only to please her husband, that Elisabeth is cold and dead inside. The husband visits the island, and the film leaves the audience confused about which of the two women he sees while he's there.

This classic art house film, one of Bergman's masterpieces, is all but impossible to describe in a few paragraphs, and it can be interpreted on multiple levels. Does Elisabeth's muteness become a kind of blank projection screen for Alma, who reverses their patient/caretaker status by casting Elisabeth in a therapist's role, then becomes enraged at what amounts to Elisabeth's breaking confidentiality? Are the women in love? Are they two sides of the same person? Is Elisabeth vampirizing Alma? How much are all of us acting; how many of us are mute about our true selves?

One could argue for and against all of the above interpretations and more. For the more narrow perspective of this book, however, I recommend that you think about the Ascendant as you watch *Persona*. Some of my own thoughts follow, but they only scratch the surface of this complex film.

The wheels of social interaction turn smoothly if we buy one another's act and accept one another's Ascendant, or at least behave as if we do. But we don't have our Ascendant working in its protective capacity all the time, particularly not when we're intimate with someone. Such a person has gotten past our Ascendant, has gotten "under our skin." In intimacy, when we're allowed to peer behind our loved one's Ascendant, we're not supposed to blab indiscriminately about what we've seen there. Elisabeth's deliberate suppression of her persona/Ascendant contributed to a feeling of intimacy with her on Alma's part, and to the subsequent dropping of Alma's own Ascendant. Then Elisabeth betrayed the confidences Alma gave her, and Alma reacted with rage. When we've shed our

Ascendant or had it stripped away, a great deal of psychological disturbance can follow.

The Development of the Ascendant

Since we aren't born with fully functioning Ascendants, when and how are they developed?

That's a good question. Here are two more: Are we ever as poised as we could possibly be? How would we know if we were?

I suspect that our Ascendants may never be completely developed, in that there's always room for more personal growth, for further integration of the Ascendant into our outward demeanor, and for further refinement of the Ascendant's expressive and protective interactions with our environment. The Ascendant can get temporarily frozen, just as people can get stuck. Yet the possibility of further growth always exists, though in some cases it's far more or less likely than in others.

Perhaps the Ascendant's early development follows a symbolic planetary path through the inner planets. We learn to communicate, with facial expressions, gestures or words (Mercury). We learn to recognize other people, to smile at them and play with them (Venus). We learn that we are different from those other people, that we are not one with Mother, that we have our own will (Mars—the "terrible twos." Mars is the natural ruler of the first house). We venture away from Mother's side and explore (Jupiter). We start school, with its structures and requirements and rules (Saturn).

Over the past several years, at the annual NORWAC (Northwest Astrology) conference in Seattle, WA, astrologer Diana Stone has given a wonderfully illuminating series of lectures about the psychodynamics of the rising sign. Copies of those lectures are available on cassette from www.astrologyetal.com, and I heartily recommend them all. Stone has developed a model that can be easily applied to any astrological configuration, not just to the Ascendant.

I also recommend her chapter, "A Communication Model for Astrologers," in the book *Communicating the Horoscope* (ed. Noel Tyl, Llewellyn: St. Paul, MN, 1995). Stone is expanding that model for an upcoming book titled *The Counseling Astrologer's Guidebook: a Ten-Step Model for Communicating the Horoscope.* Meanwhile, her profiles of the signs can be downloaded from her website, www.dianastone.com. For the purposes of this book, however, and with Stone's permission, we'll consider her model only in relation to the Ascendant.

To paraphrase Stone, she proposes that the early development of the Ascendant occurs as a response to some issue or experience in our early environment—typically our childhood and the family in which we were raised—and that those issues and experiences *lie within the archetypal energies of the Ascendant's sign.* Stone's lecture tapes cover various decisions that different rising signs may have made in response to their early environment, and the various behaviors and life situations to which such decisions may lead. They're a practical, insightful and important contribution to our knowledge about the Ascendant.

Let's consider an example. Stone says she used to think, when she saw a client with Cancer rising, that since Cancer refers to nurturing and parenting and safety in a nest, therefore that person must have had a warm and fuzzy mother and optimal nurturing as a child. Upon communicating with clients with Cancer rising about their life histories, however, Stone found instead that they often reported early experiences that tended to center more around a perceived *lack* of such nurturing. In response to those experiences, the clients then made a decision to turn themselves into the good mother that they hadn't had. "Somebody has to be the mother around here, and I guess I'm it." They might well use their Ascendants to nurture everyone and everything around them—and appear in Stone's office years later complaining that they had to take care of everyone and never got enough back in return.

I'd like to add that such people might decide, instead, that the world was so unsafe that they would nurture only themselves, and arrive in the astrologer's office years later complaining that they felt isolated and unable to shed the Cancer shell. Or they might decide to move through the world demanding that everyone nurture them, that everyone play Good Mommy to their Baby—and show up in the astrologer's office complaining that people say they're too clingy and always leave them.

I agree that the Ascendant develops with our *experiences* and *our reactions to those experiences.* I would add that it also develops with our *actions.* Mars is the natural ruler of the first house, and the sign naturally associated with the first house is Aries. I suspect that the "terrible twos," when Mars makes its first return to its natal position, is instrumental in the early development of the Ascendant. I also suspect that not only the transits, progressions and solar arcs involving the Ascendant, but also all of our Mars returns, which occur about every two years, can be critical in the continued evolution of our Ascendant.

If you free-associate about the astrological Mars, what words come to mind? Will. Desire. Motion. Boundaries. Action. Astrologer Stephen Arroyo has called the Ascendant "the identity in action." The Ascendant is about our *behavior.* Think of it as astrological behavior modification suggestions—if we modify our behavior according to our Ascendants, we feel centered, grounded and confident. We have good boundaries. We are able to act freely. Our personas are working with us and for us, not against us.

We'll spend some more time discussing the persona in Chapter Two. But first, if you're a practicing astrologer or a student and you want to take these ideas further, here are some suggestions. Please consider writing down your answers to these exercises wherever possible, so that you can start building a collection of examples to use with your clients.

1. Go to a party and guess what people's Ascendants are. Later, if you can verify your guesses in a non-intrusive manner, find out if you were right.

2. Develop the idea of Ascendant as the "mouth" of the chart. What sort of experiential food does Aries rising need? What do its teeth look like? Make a list for each rising sign. Then go back and add a different planet to each first house. How would the diet and the teeth change for an Aries Ascendant with Venus in the first house? With Saturn there?

3. Have some fun with the idea of the Ascendant as the spaceship. What does a Gemini spaceship look like? Its windows? Its armaments? Its landing gear? How about a Scorpio spaceship? Jot down some ideas for each rising sign. Then add a planet to each sign and amend its spaceship's characteristics.

4. Use an astrological computer program to calculate all of your Mars returns (or as many as you can stand to contemplate). Consider what each Mars return may have had to do with the development of your own Ascendant.

5. Watch the two movies I've mentioned, *Nell* and *Persona,* preferably in the company of another astrologer or astrologers, and discuss them. If you can think of some other movies that might concern themes or issues pertaining to the Ascendant, watch them with your astro-buddies, too.

CHAPTER TWO: THE ASCENDANT AND C.G. JUNG'S CONCEPT OF THE PERSONA

This chapter owes a great deal to the work of astrologer and Jungian analyst, Liz Greene, and the late astrologer, Richard Idemon. At one of their conferences in the 1980s, I first heard a discussion of the Ascendant's relationship to the psychologist C.G. Jung's ideas about the persona. There's not a one-on-one correspondence between the astrological Ascendant and the psychological persona. However, there are some fascinating and illuminating parallels that can deepen our understanding not only of the Ascendant, but also of the Descendant and of the entire Ascendant-Descendant axis.

Remember that the Sun represents one's sanity, one's ego or ego-complex in the sense that a psychologist would use the word. The Sun is our sense of being a self-aware person who is separate and distinct from other people. The Sun is our identity, the part of us who is most typically in the driver's seat of the psyche.

The persona is the mask that we wear in the world. The word "persona" comes from the name for the masks that actors in classical dramas wore. It could function as a kind of megaphone, to amplify the actor's voice and make it more audible in the back of the theatre. Sometimes that mask signified what sort of role the character played, and sometimes that role was a recognizable type or a stock character, or a member of the collective "chorus."

In "Definitions," from *Psychological Types* (*Collected Works* 6, Princeton, NJ: Bollingen, 1967), Jung says that the persona is an *adopted attitude* (italics mine), and:

> "the real individuality is different . . . The persona is
> thus a functional complex that comes into existence
> for reasons of adaptation or personal convenience, but
> is by no means identical with the individuality. The
> persona is exclusively concerned with the relation to

objects. The relation of the individual to the object must be sharply distinguished from the relation to the subject. By the "subject" I mean first all of those vague, dim stirrings, feelings, thoughts and sensations which flow in on us not from any demonstrable continuity of conscious experience of the object, but well up like a disturbing, inhibiting, or at times helpful influence from the dark inner depths, from the background and underground vaults of consciousness, and constitute, in their totality, our perception of the life of the unconscious. The subject, conceived of the "inner object," *is* the unconscious. Just as there is a relation to the outer object, an outer attitude, there is a relation to the inner object, an inner attitude. It is readily understandable that this inner attitude, by reason of its extremely intimate and inaccessible nature, is far more difficult to discern than the outer attitude, which is immediately perceived by everyone."

What does that passage mean? Here's my understanding of Jung's ideas as expounded in the section I just quoted. My opinions or comments about those ideas, *only as they relate to astrology*, follow each point and are in parentheses or brackets.

First, Jung states that the persona is not the individuality. (The Ascendant is not the Sun, although I doubt there's a one-on-one correspondence between the astrological Sun and what Jung would call the individuality.)

Second, Jung says that the persona is an adopted, constructed attitude, a functional adaption. (So, in a great many ways, is the Ascendant, although *the raw material from which that attitude is constructed*—the rising sign and any first house planets—*is innate.*)

Third, Jung holds that the persona is concerned *only* with our relationship to the world of objects, our outer attitude toward the external, objective world that lies outside the self. (I have several comments and opinions here, so for clarity's sake, I'll number them:

1. The Ascendant is primarily concerned with our "foreign relations," our relations to the outside world.

2. The Ascendant adapts to the outside world, the world of the object, in a particular way partly *because of the nature of the inner world*, which is in part the world of the subjective unconscious.

3. The Ascendant adapts to the outside world in a particular way not only because of the nature of the unconscious, but also *because of the nature of the rest of the chart*—of which the person may or may not be aware.

4. The Ascendant makes such adaptations in order to protect or to express the rest of the chart.

5. We can't tell by merely looking at a chart whether its owner is conscious or unconscious of its various configurations, nor with what degree of awareness or unawareness. Consciousness is an active, dynamic state and therefore is subject to change, whether that change is regression or growth.)

Let's take our discussion of Jung's thought a bit further, but before we do, remember that the Ascendant has its astrological opposite: the cusp of the seventh house, the Descendant.

The Descendant is the sign that was *setting* at the moment of birth. The seventh house is the traditional "house of marriage." It's the house of intimacy. We feel that the qualities of the seventh house cusp and any planets in that house complement us, that they fit us, that they are an important and apparently missing part of our puzzle. When we meet someone who embodies our seventh house qualities, we almost invariably respond to that person, often with strong liking or love. If we project some of our own disowned traits upon him or her, perhaps we respond with intense dislike—this house is also the traditional "house of open enemies."

We are never indifferent to someone who strongly embodies our seventh house energies. Why? Because the Ascendant and Descendant form an axis: the house of the self, and the house of the other. They form an opposition, an aspect of heightened mutual awareness and a need for balance, as if they were two people sitting on either end of a see-saw.

If the first house has some correspondence to Jung's concept of the persona, then could the seventh house also be considered in the light of Jungian thought? And could such considerations help our understanding of the astrological Ascendant?

I think the answer to both of those questions is yes, although it bears repeating that the Ascendant is not exactly the same thing as the Jungian persona. Here's Jung again (from "Definitions" in *Psychological Types, Collected Works 6*, Princeton, NJ: Bollingen, 1967):

> The inner personality is the way one behaves in relation to one's inner psychic processes; it is the inner attitude, the characteristic face, that is turned towards the unconscious. I call the outer attitude, the outward face, the *persona*; the inner attitude, the inward face, I call the *anima*.

In the case of a woman, Jung calls this inner attitude or inward face the *animus*. In the case of either a man or a woman, this inner figure is usually of the opposite sex. It also represents that person's inner image of the feminine or the masculine. According to Jung, the anima or animus governs one's relations to the *inner* world, much as the persona governs one's relations to the *outer* world.

Does that mean that the seventh house represents one's anima or animus, and that it governs our relationship to our inner world?

Yes and no and sometimes, in my opinion. I'm not a psychologist; I'm just discussing Jung's ideas for the light they can throw on the astrological Ascendant.

Let's develop these concepts further. Stay with me: here's another important idea from Jung, which I'll deliver in chunks of quotations followed by my comments or opinions.

> "*To the degree that the world invites the individual to identify with the mask,* he is delivered over to influences from within." ("The Relations between the Ego and the Unconscious," *Two Essays, Collected Works 7*, Princeton, NJ: Bollingen, 1967. Italics mine.)

Below, you'll read what Jung says can happen, first stated in general and abstract terms, when one is "delivered over to influences from within:"

> "*Identity* with the persona automatically leads to an unconscious identity with the anima because, when the ego is not differentiated from the persona, it can have no conscious relation to the unconscious processes. Consequently, it *is* these processes, it is identical with them. Anyone who is himself his outward role will infallibly succumb to the inner processes; he will either frustrate his outward role by absolute inner necessity or else reduce it to absurdity, by a process of *enantiodromia*. He can no longer keep to his individual way, and his life runs into one deadlock after another. Moreover, the anima is inevitably projected upon a real object, with which he gets into a relation of almost total dependence. Every reaction displayed by this object has an immediate,

inwardly enervating effect on the subject."
("Definitions," *Psychological Types, Collected Works*
6, Princeton, NJ: Bollingen, 1967.)

"Enantiodromia," a word in the passage quoted above, means the tendency for one extreme to flip into its opposite: e.g., the sexual Puritan participates in an orgy; the rabid atheist has an overwhelming religious conversion, etc.
In the following section, Jung gives some more specific and concrete examples of what can happen when we overidentify with our masks. It's the longest and the last quotation from Jung in this chapter, and its ideas are important to our discussion of the Ascendant. After the quotation, I'll explain why.

> "The construction of a collectively suitable persona means a formidable concession to the external world, a genuine self-sacrifice which (can) drive the ego straight into identification with the persona, so that people really do exist who believe they are what they pretend to be. The "soullessness" of such an attitude is, however, only apparent, for under no circumstances will the unconscious tolerate this shifting of the centre of gravity. When we examine such cases critically, we find that the excellence of the mask is compensated by the "private life" going on behind it . . . Whoever builds up too good a persona for himself naturally has to pay for it with irritability. Bismarck had hysterical weeping fits, Wagner indulged in correspondence about the belts of his silk dressing-gowns, Nietzsche wrote letters to his "dear lama," . . . etc. But there are subtler things than the banal lapses of heroes. I once made the acquaintance of a very venerable personage—in fact, one might

easily call him a saint. I stalked around him for three whole days, but never a mortal failing did I find in him. My feeling of inferiority grew ominous, and I was beginning to think seriously of how I might better myself. Then, on the fourth day, his wife came to consult me . . . Well, nothing of the sort has ever happened to me before or since. But this I did learn: that any man who becomes one with his persona can cheerfully let all disturbances manifest themselves through his wife without her noticing it, though she pays for her self-sacrifice with a bad neurosis.

These identifications with a social role are a very fruitful source of neuroses. A man cannot get rid of himself in favour of an artificial personality without punishment. Even the attempt to do so brings on, in all ordinary cases, unconscious reactions in the form of bad moods, affects, phobias, compulsive ideas, backslidings, vices, etc. The socially "strong man" is in his private life often a mere child where his own states of feeling are concerned; his public discipline (which he demands quite particularly of others) goes miserably to pieces in private. His "happiness in his work" assumes a woeful countenance at home; his "spotless" public morality looks strange indeed behind the mask . . . and the wives of such men would have a pretty tale to tell. As to his selfless altruism, his children have decided views about that." ("The Relations between the Ego and the Unconscious," *Two Essays on Analytical Psychology, Collected Works 7*, Princeton, NJ: Bollingen, 1967.)

Why are we delving into this Jungian material?

Because of its key concept *that if we over-identify with our personas or our Ascendants, we are headed for trouble in several ways.*

First, we risk losing contact with part or all of our deeper selves, whether we are conscious of those deeper selves or not, and whether or not those deeper selves are represented by the Sun or the Moon or some large stellium.

Second, we risk succumbing to knee-jerk, compulsive attractions or antipathies—remember that one name for the seventh house is "the house of open enemies"?—to anyone who strongly embodies our Descendant's energies. Such attractions can and do occur whether the people who trigger them embody our seventh house energies in a healthy way or not.

Third, we risk unconsciously assigning our partners the role of our projected seventh house energies, and risk driving them into a less than optimal manifestation of that role. Sooner or later, most healthy people will rebel against such an assignment, which is detrimental to the wholeness of both parties. But if we're still too identified with our first house energies, we don't know enough about our deep selves, and/or we are projecting our seventh house energies, then when our partner breaks character with that projected role, we can become profoundly disturbed. We can feel, consciously or not, that not only is the relationship threatened, but so is some part of our own vital core. And, in a way, we are correct—if the only way we've been able to connect with that part of our own core was by having our partner carry it for us.

Our Ascendants, our masks, protect us and express us, but we overidentify with them at our own peril. Relationships can bring us face to face with the attractive or repellent Other, with that which is not ourselves, at least as we first experience that dynamic with the Other. Actually, relationships *first* bring us face to face with *that which is not our mask.* By relating consciously to that Other, we can attain greater wholeness. We can better understand what is our mask, what is our identity, and how the two interact with one another and with other people.

Therefore, understanding our masks—our Ascendants—can also involve understanding their opposites—our Descendants—and why those opposites can be attractive *or* repellent. We'll spend more time on that concept on an Ascendant-by-Ascendant basis in the Cookbook section of this book.

Let's move on to Chapter Three, and learn what the world of the theater can teach us about the Ascendant.

But first, if you're a practicing astrologer or a student and you want to take the ideas discussed in this chapter a bit further, here are some suggestions. Some of these exercises contain such complex ideas that you could spend years thinking about them, so don't expect to reach any swift conclusions. Just let yourself begin to consider them. You may even want to review each chapter's exercises after you've finished reading the entire book.

1. How does your persona feel different from your individual ego?

2. How is your attitude toward the world different from your attitude toward your inner life?

3. List three qualities you profoundly like in other people, and that you want in a friend or a closer relationship. Then list three qualities you profoundly *dislike* in others and do not want in a friend or a more intimate relationship. How many of each of those qualities do you actually have yourself? How does each quality relate to your Ascendant or Descendant? If you're drawing a blank about your own life, ask the same questions about a friend whose chart you know well.

4. Think about when, over the course of your life, you've been the most identified with the energies of your Ascendant and, at the same time, most out of touch with the rest of your chart. What were your relationships like—all of them, not just your romantic ones—during those periods? Were you possibly drawing extreme versions of your

Descendant energy into your life? (Relationship issues can of course come from many other sources in one's chart and one's life, but for this exercise, we're considering just the Ascendant-Descendant axis.)

5. If exercise four is difficult to consider in your own life, do you know someone who seems to have the same persistent issues in relationships? It's always the same script with him or her, just with different actors or actresses. If you know what this person's Ascendant is, think about his or her patterns as they might relate to his or her Ascendant *and* Descendant.

6. When have you had the most busy, active outer life and were known (personally, not just by reputation) by the greatest number of people? What was your surface self like then? Did you identify with that surface self? How did it affect your inner life?

7. If you're drawing a blank on exercise six, think about it for the most prominent, famous or popular person whom you know personally. Of course, not all such people overidentify with their personas or project their own traits onto their partners. But some of them occasionally do. As the proverb says, "No man is a hero to his valet." What is this famous person like with his or her intimates, face to face?

8. What the public most wants to know about famous people is something about their private lives, about what they are like in person. Magazines sell lots of issues by publishing articles such as "Ms. Renowned Celebrity At Home "or "Mr. Box Office Draw, Up Close and Personal." When someone has a very polished and famous persona, we want to know what lies beneath it. Why might that be?

CHAPTER THREE: ACTING AND THE ASCENDANT

I once heard the late Richard Idemon tell a story about a client of his, an actress who had Neptune conjunct her Ascendant. She was in character on a set, and when her husband came to visit her, *he walked right past her without recognizing her.*

Especially on the Ascendant or in the first house, Neptune, the Lord of Consciousness, can be a bit like Proteus: infinitely flexible and able to adopt a multitude of forms. Why? Because Neptune is the part of you that experiences yourself as something other than an ego, a body or a personality. Neptune is our experience of *sheer consciousness* and as such, it can be very unidentified with the body and with the Ascendant. Neptune on the Ascendant can make for a very fluid mask, as that actress's husband would be quick to agree.

Far more than memorizing one's lines is involved in the art of acting. Some schools of thought in dramatic art refer to the body as "the instrument" (particularly schools deriving from the work of Constantin Stanislavski and his "method of physical actions," often called Method acting). The actor plays the "instrument" of the body to create a role, using not just dialog but also body language, tone of voice, posture, gestures, facial expressions, etc. Some actors stay in character whenever they're on the set, and refuse to answer if addressed by their own names. Some actors alter their bodies by gaining or losing a lot of weight to play different roles.

Far more than our speech is involved with our Ascendants. As Emerson said, "What you do speaks so loudly that I cannot hear what you say." Do you doubt it? Then try something I suggest to fiction writing students: rent a *well-reviewed* movie (which is more likely to have good acting) that you've never seen. A film with some treachery and double-dealing and plot twists would be ideal. Watch the movie with the sound turned all the way down. One of the dictums of creative writing is "show, don't tell." A good film minus its sound will demonstrate to you how the performance of a skilled actor "shows" rather than just "tells."

While you're watching that movie, make some notes. Who are these characters? Who likes whom? Who's lying? Who's conflicted? Who has something up his sleeve? Then watch it again with the sound turned up. You'll probably be surprised at how right you were.

Let's return to the questions: "Who's lying?;" "Who's conflicted?;" and "Who has something up his sleeve?" If your answers were right, *how could you tell?* If you were wrong, *how did you miss it?*

Consider an example from the film *The Lord of the Rings: The Fellowship of the Ring.* After the Fellowship survives an avalanche, and Frodo discovers he's lost the Ring in the snow, Boromir *says* the right things when he gives the Ring back: "Of course. It's yours. I care not." He even laughs, and ruffles Frodo's hair. But mere seconds ago, Boromir was staring at the Ring with hunger and fascination in his eyes. He responds too slowly to Aragorn's command to give the Ring to Frodo, and his laugh is forced. Boromir's behavior, his appearance, his tone of voice and his body language *are incongruent with what he says.* They betray an inner conflict. Also, they are incongruent with the outer situation: Frodo is the rightful Ring-Bearer, not Boromir. We, the audience, sense that something is wrong when Boromir is so reluctant to return the Ring. We no longer trust him. And we shouldn't: he's being tempted by the Ring, and not much time will pass before he tries to take it from Frodo by force.

Here's a more subtle example, from the film *Body Heat.* As the movie progresses, some, but not all, of the audience probably begin to suspect Kathleen Turner's character, Matty, of seducing William Hurt's character, small-town lawyer Ned Racine, in order to have Ned take the fall for murdering Matty's rich husband. Matty gets away with a fortune, while Ned gets a jail sentence. Those viewers who suspected Matty might have started to wonder when she tells her smitten lover Ned about her husband. She says, "He's not at all like you. I can't stand the thought of him. He's small and mean and weak." It isn't so much what she says, but *how she says it.* She's weeping, but not very hard, and her description of her husband comes out in complete sentences, not particularly broken by sobs. Ned totally buys her story, however, probably partly because Matty is so passionate—so congruent—when she's in bed with him.

The most chilling bad guys are the ones we can't read, the ones who maintain a perfect or near-perfect surface all along, right up to the unmistakable revelation that they are not what they seem. Consider another example, from the film *No Way Out.* Only at the very end of that spy thriller do we discover that Kevin Costner's character is a double agent. We're very surprised, too, because his character's persona had been so believable, so congruent. There weren't any inconsistencies in his character's behavior, speech, gestures or facial expressions. Therefore, the revelation at the end of this movie packs quite a wallop, more so than if we'd suspected Costner's character all along.

Some of what's true in the movies also applies to real life. What happens when a person, not an actor, has an Ascendant that is incongruent with his insides or with his surroundings? Others either get a sense that something is off-kilter and mistrust that person, or they so misread him that misunderstandings and even trouble are likely to follow.

Our Ascendants can't express our entire selves, nor should they. That's not their job. But they should protect or express our inner selves well enough, and deal with the outside world well enough, that mistrust or misinterpretations don't routinely occur.

Want some examples from real life, rather than the cinema? I have three friends, two men and a woman, who have Aries Ascendants. Very different people, they nevertheless have one thing in common. With the mask of the Warrior, the initial impressions that all three give are a bit scary. None of them looks remotely like Arnold Schwarzenegger, but there's a foreboding aura around each of them.

You feel cautious upon first meeting them, as if you should treat them with respect, as if they might possibly be dangerous. They all give an impression of energy held tautly in check, and that could be suddenly and even violently released at any second.

I'd seen one of the men around town for years before I met him face to face, and I'd given him a wide berth whenever I could. When I made friends with these three people, however, I found protective instincts and refreshing directness and liveliness beneath those alarming masks. I also learned that they were fairly aware of the initial impact they made on others. One of the men told me, "It's a good thing to look frightening in a dark parking lot at two in the morning, but otherwise I get tired of being misunderstood. I've worked hard to seem more approachable when I first meet people." As for the woman, when I met her I discovered a longtime running joke among her friends that her alter ego is a "Klingon chick," from the warrior race in the *Star Trek* television series, and that she faces new or challenging situations as that Klingon chick.

Note that my friends learned when it might be wise to use their Aries Ascendants, and when it might be wise to soften them. How did they learn? By their experiences with other people. By interacting with the world around them.

There aren't any simple answers to that question, but we can perhaps start to address it further by considering the craft of acting. You can well imagine how important it is for actors to be able to change their personas consciously, and to have a great deal of control over that process.

In order not to prejudice myself and my questions and reactions, *before* I read work by Stanislavksi and his intellectual descendants, I interviewed some actors and directors and asked them to talk about how they got out of their own skins and into their characters' skins. None of the actors I interviewed are astrologers, and none of them knew very much about astrology in general or the Ascendant in particular.

One very experienced professional director and actress, who's also a playwright and an acting teacher, began her response by saying flatly, "If it's not rooted in the actor's own body, it's a trick." She continued, "To find (the character's) true movement on stage is to find your own true movement, *if you were in that character's shoes.*"

"How do you do that?" I asked.

"Be comfortable in your own body. Know your own body," said the director. "I get my students to stop using assumed or stock gestures or mannerisms, like waving their fists if the character's angry. Instead, I ask them to think about what they do and how they move when *they're* really angry." She grinned. "And if they don't remember, their friends will. I might magnify or reduce a gesture of theirs, or move it to another part of their body. But it's still *their* gesture, their own movement, not some stereotyped gesture as if they were in a farce or a melodrama. If they overact like that," she continued, "they're hiding for some reason, sometimes a painful one. So I wait until I've gotten to know my students and they feel comfortable with me before I correct overacting."

One actress I interviewed has extensive community theater experience and a background in radio and journalism. She said: "I'm certainly no expert on Method acting, but I think of it as immersing myself in a role, especially on an emotional level. One interesting thing I've discovered, however, is how much adopting OUTER characteristics of the person I'm playing can sometimes help jump-start me into the feelings. In other words, while my inclination is to try to imagine a character's feelings first, and then figure out how to embody them, sometimes doing physical things first frees me up emotionally—and vice versa!

"Sometimes, even for auditions, I dress the part, if possible. That also helps me get into character, and I think most actors would agree that once they don their costumes for dress rehearsals, a new energy or greater sense of this alternate reality we're portraying really enters in.

"My favorite compliment following a performance is 'I couldn't believe that was YOU up there!' That tells me that I have succeeded in embodying my character. The best compliment I ever got from a fellow actor was something like this: 'What I admire about you is that every time I've been in a play with you or seen you in one, you've seemed completely different than you did in your previous roles.' Wow—how gratifying."

This woman's next comments were particularly interesting in light of her natal Neptune-Venus opposition. She has a twelfth house Neptune that makes a wide conjunction to her Ascendant. "Sometimes after a show, I have trouble 'switching over' to being myself again. For instance, if I'm in a drama that ends on a serious note, it takes me a while to feel the levity of others who want to go out and party after a show. Or, if I played a comic role and had a blast doing it, my energy may be high and my wit quicker and sharper than usual (i.e., the 'buzz' lingers), but there's also a significant chance that I'll feel drained and like I just want to go home. Finally, I truly feel a letdown after a run ends. I hate it! Since I became that character to the best of my ability, i.e., brought as much of myself to it as would be helpful for the role, I feel like I'm losing a part of myself once the production is over."

Another actress, British by birth and with a practical temperament, told me, "I don't really know what 'Method' acting is. It's not the way I was trained. I think it was Richard Burton who said, 'Make sure you hit your mark and try not to bump into the furniture.' With the really good actors, I think there is a lot more technical expertise and a lot less mysticism." Nevertheless, this woman added, "I find it hard to find my character until I decide what I am going to wear. For some reason that helps me 'place' the character, so I decide this very early in the process."

Are you detecting the common theme of using *externals*—one's physical body, gestures and clothing—to convey a character's inner state? That may seem like a paradox, but think of it this way: it's as if *the actress's Ascendant has to take on an imprint of the character's Ascendant* in order to play that character well. Again, our Ascendants both *protect* the rest of the chart and *express* it. Perhaps, for an actor to be convincing, he or she has to replicate the character's Ascendant by using his or her own Ascendant and his or her own body.

Before we continue to Chapter Four, here are some ways to expand your consideration of this material:

1. Find a copy of *How to Read a Person Like a Book*, by Gerard Nierenberg. This book is a good discussion of the body language shared by many if not all Americans. Remember, however, that there are vast cultural differences in body language.

2. If you have friends in law enforcement, particularly a detective or an interrogator, ask them how they can tell if someone is lying.

3. If you have a friend who's a therapist, ask him or her the same question.

4. If you have a friend who's a professional body worker or a yoga instructor, ask what patterns of physical tension might correlate with certain feelings or personality types.

5. If you have friends who are actors or actresses, conduct your own interview with them, and ask how they prepare for a role.

6. If you're an astrologer who sees clients, think carefully about how your own Ascendant might protect or express the rest of your chart. How can you use the energy of your Ascendant to put people at ease and establish rapport? What qualities of your Ascendant might be off-putting for some people, and how can you tone them down? How can you use the energy of your clients' Ascendants to establish rapport?

7. For some professional and helpful feedback on your Ascendant, check out your local continuing education courses. The director/actress/playwright/teacher whom I mentioned earlier teaches a communication class for business people. Using acting techniques, she helps her business students figure out what mannerisms and

gestures they're using, which ones don't work, and how to change them in order to become more persuasive and effective.

CHAPTER FOUR: THE ASCENDANT AND "STYLE"

Style? What do we mean by that word?

I almost called this chapter "The Ascendant and Clothing," but "style" is more inclusive, and more applicable to the concepts I'll discuss here.

In the context of the Ascendant, I mean your *personal* style, in the sense of your "vibes," to use a 1960s word, or your "energy," to use a New Age word. How well do you handle yourself out in the world? Are you poised? Are you awkward? Can you think on your feet? What first impressions do you give? If we want to stretch the word further, cultures have "styles," too. I've lived in the South most of my life, and the South's cultural, interpersonal and conversational style is very different from that of the Northeast or California. Nor is American cultural style like that of the French.

To some extent, I also mean the word "style" as *In Style* magazine would use it: your clothing sense and the overall impact that your appearance makes. We can draw lots of interesting connections between the Ascendant and clothing.

Consider the following proverbs or one-liners:

A wolf in sheep's clothing.
You can't judge a book by its cover.
Your face is your fortune.
Beauty is only skin deep.
Pretty is as pretty does.
Fool for a pretty face.
Clothes make the man.

How about a few book titles?

What You Wear Can Change Your Life
Dress for Success

What Not To Wear for Every Occasion
Frumpy to Foxy in 15 Minutes Flat

The Ascendant is like our astrological costume. It's the energy uniform that our chart wears. It's also the energy uniform that we *should* wear, in order for our mask to be healthy, to protect the rest of the chart sometimes, and to express it at other times.

Do modern Westerners wear the same clothing every single day? Of course not. Why do you change your clothes? If the only considerations we applied to clothing were hygienic, we'd have far smaller wardrobes. Among many other purposes, we use clothing to signal something about our mood, role, status, rank, sexuality, intentions, and sociopolitical leanings.

Think of the sign of your Ascendant, metaphorically, as your basic wardrobe. The various expressions and dimensions of that sign might be different articles of clothing within that wardrobe. Any other signs and/or planets in your first house are still more costumes in that wardrobe. Part of developing a healthy, well-working Ascendant is knowing what outfit within its wardrobe, as described by the signs and planets in your first house, to employ for what occasion.

You have Pisces rising. You're teaching a yoga class. No problem, you can use a classic metaphorical outfit in your Pisces rising wardrobe: the mystic. If you like concrete images, you might visualize that Pisces rising costume as full of gently draping blue, lavender and silver panels of shimmering fabric. But after class, some of your students haven't folded up their mats or put away their blocks and cushions. You put on your first house Mars in Aries outfit—if you want a concrete image, maybe it's a red leather belt with a sharp sword and a shield—and ask your students to put their props away. You might ask politely, or gently, or humorously, because that Mars in Aries is still being filtered through your Pisces Ascendant. *But you do ask*—if you've learned how to use your first house Aries Mars.

Meanwhile, your friend Jane has Sagittarius rising, with Saturn in Capricorn in her first house. What clothing images would fit Sagittarius rising? Indiana Jones in well-worn, dusty travel gear. A gypsy's flashy costume, with long dangling earrings and multilayered skirts and a red rose clenched between the teeth. A cowboy's chaps and spurs and lariat and hat. A WWI flying ace's helmet and goggles and scarf. A scholar's cap and gown.

What about clothing images for Saturn in Capricorn? A CEO's three piece pinstriped suit. A hermit's plain and functional garb, including a Swiss army knife. Low-heeled black pumps, pearl stud earrings. Conservative classics in muted shades of grey or navy or brown.

The Sagittarian and Capricorn images don't seem to fit with one another. But if Jane has Sagittarius rising with a first house Saturn in Capricorn, *she needs both types of energies.* Sometimes the verve and élan of Sagittarius will deal with the outside world for her; sometimes the shrewd efficiency of Saturn in Capricorn will be her foreign ambassador, and sometimes a blend of the two needs to manifest. Jane's Sagittarius Ascendant might love to climb Mount Everest—and those practical Saturn skills might save Jane's life during the ascent.

What about aspects from other planets to the Ascendant, planets that are not in the first house? They can be felt or sensed through the Ascendant, although not so strongly as an in-your-face first house planet is felt or sensed. It's more as if the aspecting planet's energy is leaking out around the edges of the Ascendant, or as if we can glimpse it behind someone's mask.

To continue our clothing metaphor, think of aspecting planets as something like *accessories* to that mask. The nature of the aspect (square, trine, etc.) implies how comfortable the person is with showing that planetary energy, and also how comfortable the outside world is with perceiving that planetary energy.

As a friend says, "Accessories *make* an outfit."

Time for some examples. A friend whose Cancer Sun and Pisces Moon both trine his Scorpio Ascendant is one of the best and most perceptive listeners I know, and he remembers everything about everyone. Most Scorpio Ascendants can scrutinize you like a cross between a laser beam and a can opener, and he's no exception. Unlike most Scorpio Ascendants, however, in his case it's very hard to find that focused attention threatening. Finally I realized why: his Scorpio Ascendant's ability to perceive others deeply and to be direct with them is softened by a trine from a nurturing Cancer Sun, and warmed by a trine from an accepting Pisces Moon.

My husband Steven and our colleague, astrologer Jeffrey Wolf Green, both have Scorpio rising too, with Pluto squaring their Ascendants. Very different in other ways, Steven and Jeffrey share a Plutonian intensity, directness and frankness. Like most Scorpio Ascendants, they're both well aware of the tragic dimension of life and the darker recesses within the human psyche, which they can discuss with a bluntness that milder souls may find alarming—that's their Plutos squaring their Ascendants. One day, to Steven and Jeffrey's great Plutonian glee, they learned that someone at an astrology conference who was watching the two of them walk by had muttered, "There go the Death Brothers."

Personally, as Steven's wife, Jeffrey's friend, and the editor of their *Measuring the Night* books, I find the intensity of the "Death Brothers," their willingness to cut to the chase, both refreshing and engagingly honest. It makes me think of a poem by the great Russian poet, Anna Akhmatova (from *Twenty Poems*, trans. Jane Kenyon, Eighties Press and Alley Press: St Paul, MN, 1990):

It is not with the lyre of someone in love
that I go seducing people.
The rattle of the leper
is what sings in my hands.

If you had an immediate positive reaction to that poem, then I can almost guarantee that you have a strong Pluto or a lot of Scorpio or a prominent Eighth House in your birth chart. The "rattle of the leper" of a square from Pluto can be a useful accessory for a Scorpio Ascendant. It *expresses* the depth and intensity within that person. It also *protects* that person's inner life, particularly from people who wouldn't handle his or her intensity very well.

What if Pluto were sextiling or trining someone's Scorpio Ascendant? That person might not carry a lyre—we are talking about Pluto, after all. It might be a loud electric guitar, or a big onyx ring in an elaborately carved silver setting, or a particularly penetrating gaze. But it wouldn't be the rattle of a leper.

As the jewelry ad says, *"Now* you're dressed."

I don't know if the notion I'll outline in this paragraph originated with Richard Idemon, but I first heard it at one of his seminars. He pointed out that the twelfth house has a womb-like, enclosed, hidden sort of energy, while the first house is more like birth, when we first physically separate from our mothers. It makes sense that the Ascendant correlates with birth: the Ascendant is the sign that was rising when you took your first breath, and astrologers need your exact birth time in order to determine your Ascendant correctly. Idemon theorized that the Ascendant can be seen as a reaction to and against one's twelfth house energies, as an attempt to emerge into the world and not remain hidden in the womb-like or regression-prone twelfth house. For example, if someone has Pisces on the twelfth house cusp and Aries rising, their Aries demeanor seems to say, "I am *not* spacy! I am *not* a marshmallow!"

To the best of my knowledge, Steven and I first came up with the next idea. The fifth house makes a natural trine to the Ascendant, and it's associated with pleasures, creativity and performance. Once you've broken the ice with people to the degree that they relax around you and can start to feel playful, you may notice their fifth house energies at work, almost like a second and more light-hearted

Ascendant. The fifth house is how you "perform" for an audience whom you've allowed to come a bit closer to you, a bit within the outermost defenses of your Ascendant. If your audience is receptive, you know you made a good judgment in allowing them to come closer. Maybe one day you'll let them into your seventh house.

I have a fifth house Neptune trining my Ascendant, but I have to feel fairly comfortable around someone before I reveal how non-linear and absent-minded and silly I can be. Steven has Aries on his fifth house cusp. Once his office hours are over, his friends and I have learned to expect a certain amount of rough-and-tumble teasing. A friend with a fifth house Aries Sun saves her fire-breathing political rants for her close friends. (Once her Scorpio husband told me how much he loves it when she gets on her soapbox. She married well!)

This chapter wouldn't be complete without some philosophical and speculative observations about the Ascendant, clothing, and women in particular. Please remember that I refer to modern Western culture, simply because that's the one I've observed the most.

One of my favorite *Doonesbury* cartoons from years ago shows a female reporter handing a news story to her male editor. The editor reads, "As the Senator continued the filibuster, the statuesque father of three looked stunning in a pearl grey pinstripe with matching socks, and cufflinks by Dior." The editor stops and blinks, puzzled. Then he notices the reporter's evil grin and says, "You're trying to make a point here, aren't you?"

You have no doubt noticed that in the modern West, women can seem obsessed about their appearance, makeup and clothing. Women tend to own many more garments than men do. Women's fashions change far more frequently than men's do, and they cost more, too. Why might that be?

Personally, I don't have any answers to those questions, and I don't intend to cast any blame or make any excuses. We are sailing into controversial waters here. Still, I'd like to discuss a few different and,

I hope, interesting points of view about this topic, with the general aim of relating them to the Ascendant.

One fairly zoological school of thought might hold that since most men are very visual and very sexually responsive to a woman's appearance, perhaps women are trying to adapt to that taste in men by an endless search for more becoming clothing and makeup. Perhaps, to ensure the survival of the species in a prehistoric era when that survival was far from a given, men carry a biological drive to impregnate as many women as possible. From a biologically ideal standpoint, to help ensure the survival of the species, those women should be of an age when they are most likely to bear healthy children: about seventeen to twenty-nine years old. Meanwhile, to promote the survival of their children, perhaps women have a biological drive to make every effort to keep the children's father present. If a woman varies her appearance as much as possible and keeps looking youthful as long as she can, perhaps she'll be able to retain his interest in her and his help with her offspring.

All of the above may or may not be true, which doesn't mean "right" from any philosophical point of view. I'm speculating about biology, not ethics.

The Ascendant is that which presents us to the outside world, that which adapts and adjusts to that world. The Ascendant is a learned construct, a way of protecting and expressing the deeper self to the world outside. Until fairly recently in the modern West, for whatever reason or reasons, the world outside *was* primarily a man's world. A woman's face *was* her fortune, unless she was willing to fall within some narrowly defined roles, such as teacher, secretary, nurse, nun or prostitute. Even "actress" was suspect until quite recently. In other words, even more so than today, *a woman's appearance used to have a vital impact on the quality of her life,* an impact that can scarcely be overestimated. Our culture's habits and customs—and maybe our instincts—haven't yet adjusted to the changing times. From the perspective of modern Western civilization, those times have changed only very recently.

Our appearance and our clothing are related, and both relate to our Ascendants. No wonder women are so focused on their wardrobes.

Not only are women more often judged initially or even primarily on their appearance, women still experience tremendous social pressure to be "sweet," to develop adaptable, accomodating, gracious, selfless, cooperative and supportive masks. Often, boys are allowed to be a little rough around the edges—"Boys will be boys." Often, girls receive relentless training in manners—"It's nice to be important, but it's more important to be nice. If you can't say something nice, don't say anything at all." I suspect that women who are frowning are told by total strangers to smile far more often than frowning men are told to do so.

Mars, the natural ruler of the first house and therefore the natural ruler of the Ascendant, is more suppressed and repressed in women than it is in men, and more directed into socially acceptable channels. I surmise, therefore, that all other things being equal, most women have more trouble developing their Ascendants than men do, and therefore that more women have trouble differentiating between their identity and their Ascendants than men do.

If women can't fully and freely develop and express their Ascendants in their behavior, what do they do instead? That energy has to go somewhere. I suspect that it often goes into clothing and into body image. Women can start searching for their identity, and for the right mask to express it and protect it, *in their closets and their mirrors.*

Once a friend told me about her young teenage daughter, who said when trying on clothes, "I like this outfit. This is the first time I've really been able to see myself."

Can you imagine a teenage boy saying something like that?

My friend took a deep breath and gently told her daughter, "You've seen your *self* every day of your life, and you always will.

This is the first time you've seen a style of *clothing* that you really like to wear."

I said a moment ago that women's confusion about where the boundary lies between their deep selves and their Ascendants may be reflected in their focus on their clothing and body image. The realm of body image contains some particularly mixed messages. The April 2006 issue of *Oprah* magazine quotes a global study commissioned by Dove, whose "Campaign for Real Beauty" soap ads feature women of all sizes:

> * ninety-two percent of American women aged 15 to 64 want to change their physical appearance, most often their body weight and shape;
> * about two-thirds of American women agree that if they feel bad about themselves, it's most often because of their looks or weight;
> * almost seventy percent of women, *globally,* back out of going to school, work or a job interview because they don't feel good about their appearance.

As Western women have assumed more and more active roles in the outside world, fashion has dictated that they should be thinner and thinner— athletic, perhaps, but extremely lean. Studies indicate that fashion models used to be about 8% underweight; in 1991 they were about 23% underweight, and may be even more so today (Naomi Wolf, *The Beauty Myth*, New York: William Morrow, 1991). Models' average clothing size used to be an eight; now it's a zero. Even television newscaster Katie Couric, not a model and far from overweight, was digitally imaged to appear thinner.

Long before I read Naomi Wolf's book *The Beauty Myth*, I doubted it was an accident that both the modern women's movement and the über-bony model Twiggy burst into collective awareness in the late 1960s. Today's women are hearing at least two messages.

Whether or not they're mothers, they're supposed to be strong, independent, hardworking and productive members of society, enjoying full equality with men. Yet in order to be attractive in today's Western culture, *women's media-driven goal is to diminish themselves,* regardless of their natural build, their metabolism, and how much time they can spend at the gym. No wonder more women are getting plastic surgery. This conflict is getting visited upon women's Ascendants, wardrobes and bodies in the forms of an overemphasis upon externals, and of a corresponding diminution of their inner lives and of their sense of connectedness to one another as multidimensional, soulful *people*, not merely as bodies, costumes, competitors and roles.

Doubtless there are also men who feel caught in similar or parallel double binds. Men suffer from cultural assumptions and pressures, too—ask any man who's shorter than average. I'm not assigning any blame, and I have no "solutions." But I fear that the more our culture adheres to external and material values and de-emphasizes or denies the life of the spirit and the psyche, the more exacerbated this conflict will become for both genders, East and West.

Here are discussion points for those who want further exploration of some of the astrological material in this chapter:

1. Think carefully about your own Ascendant. What clothing images or costume metaphors can you invent for the sign on its cusp, and for any other signs or planets in your first house? If you're stuck, ask one of your astro-buddies, preferably the biggest clotheshorse among them.

2. Same question as number one for the Ascendants of at least three friends.

3. Same question for the Ascendants of at least three people whom you don't know well, but whom your clotheshorse astro-buddy does. Discuss those images with him or her.

4. Same question for the Ascendants of three famous people for whom you have accurate birth data. Stuck? Go to astrodatabank.com for some famous people's charts, or find that clothes-obsessed astro-buddy.

5. Rent some more movies and guess what the characters' Ascendants are, based on their clothing. Or guess what your favorite TV show's characters' Ascendants might be, based on their wardrobes. If you practice exercises 1 through 5 regularly, you will have all sorts of images at your fingertips when you're talking about your clients' Ascendants.

6. Try this experiment if you think entirely too much fuss is made about clothing. Dress as elegantly as you can short of a formal event, then browse at an expensive store, followed by a five and dime. Pay attention to how you're treated. Wait a couple of weeks, then dress in sloppy sweats, don't comb your hair, and go browsing at the same two stores.

7. Consider the first exercise on this list. If you have a timid client, which of your own Ascendant's "costumes," metaphorically speaking, might be most reassuring for that client? If you have a brash, fire-eating client, which of your Ascendant's "costumes" would best help you establish rapport with him or her? Now go through your closet. What actual clothing do you own that best approximates the gentle "costume" and the assertive "costume" we just talked about? Within the bounds of propriety, *wear those outfits the next time you see those people.* With practice, you can analyze your new clients' charts and your own, and not only behave but also dress in a way that may help set them at ease with you. It's not difficult, it can't hurt, and it can be a lot of fun. Our office manager can always tell if I have a new client by the way I'm dressed.

CHAPTER FIVE:
THE ASCENDANT WITH THE SUN AND THE MOON

When one first learns astrology, a big stepping stone is the analysis of the primal triad: Sun-Moon-Ascendant blends. How well do the sanity (Sun), the happiness (Moon) and the style (Ascendant) get along with one another? To put the same question another way, how well do the ego (Sun), the emotions (Moon) and the mask (Ascendant) get along? Those blends can work well or poorly, and if they work poorly, one of the three factors in the primal triad can become like the odd person out.

If the Ascendant is the odd one out, then you are not innately as comfortable with the energies of your Ascendant as you are with those of your Sun and Moon. Understanding *your initial impact on other people*, and making adjustments in your Ascendant's presentation and behavior if they are either misleading to others or depleting to your inner life, are vital to your becoming a well-integrated person. You'll have to work harder to develop your optimal persona in a pro-active, healthy way, rather than reacting to the outer world in a dysfunctional way. Otherwise, your persona won't express or protect the rest of your chart very well, and your interactions with others can become distorted. If you overdo your Ascendant, people will think you *are* no more and no less than your Ascendant. If you underdo your Ascendant, you will feel socially awkward and vulnerable. In either case, your inner life can suffer and become very isolated from the outside world.

Let's look at some examples. Feel free to simplify the signs or even make caricatures of them as you think about Sun-Moon-Ascendant blends. It's always wise to go to a simpler level of analysis when you're first thinking through a concept.

How comfortable is a cautious Cancer Ascendant handling the "foreign relations" of a man with a bold Aries Sun and Moon? Maybe the Aries Sun and Moon want to go trekking across Australia, but the

Cancer Ascendant has a hard time leaving home. How could this man settle that inner conflict? Note that as the odd one out, it's the Cancer Ascendant that has to adapt and stretch more than the Aries Sun and Moon do. Maybe our hero devotes a lot of energy to finding the perfect house sitter, so his Cancer Ascendant will have less anxiety about leaving his nest unoccupied. Maybe he invests in a state of the art tent and hiking gear, to maximize his Cancer Ascendant's comfort and safety levels. Maybe he travels with close friends who feel like family and are experienced hikers.

What if his Cancer Ascendant "wins" the conflict, and our hero stays home? Then he's in trouble. Maybe not right away, but sooner or later his Aries Sun and Moon's thwarted need to develop courage will erupt someplace else in his life. He becomes moody and irascible. He picks a fight with his mate. He wages war on his neighbors' barking dogs or noisy teenagers, when they're just being dogs or kids and haven't broken any neighborhood covenants. He gets a reputation as an irrational jerk with a hair-trigger temper—see the Cancer crab brandishing its claws on its home turf?—and his ability to connect to others and to the outside world as anything other but a cartoon of himself is impaired.

Let's reverse the signs in our example. How well does an assertive Aries Ascendant represent the inner life of a sensitive Cancer Sun and Moon? It's easy to imagine that the Aries Ascendant could be very blunt, leading people to think that our hero can take it just as well as he can dish it out. Imagine others' surprise when they hurt the feelings of the double Cancer, who then lashes out in an Aries way. How could he avoid this scenario? Again, when the Ascendant is the odd man out in the primal triad, it's the Ascendant that has to do the most adjusting. Our double Cancer with Aries rising might learn to be less reflexively abrasive, so that his Aries Ascendant doesn't overreact to perceived threats—and that Cancerian Sun and Moon energy will perceive many of them. He might dare (Aries) to go into therapy (Cancer), although it scares him, or he might take anger management classes. He might use the Aries Ascendant to carve out time for his Cancerian inner life and to defend that time from all distractions. He might look carefully at his Aries Ascendant's tendency to bite off more stress than his Cancer Sun and Moon can chew.

What if the Sun or Moon is in the same sign as the Ascendant and is in the first house, or even conjuncts the Ascendant from the first house? Those are special cases. Particularly with the conjunction, the head (Sun) or the heart (Moon) are fused with the mask (Ascendant).

Let's talk about Sun-Ascendant conjunctions first. Particularly with the Sun in the first house, with this configuration the job of the mask should be primarily expressive of the ego, rather than protective of it. What you see should be what you get. Such a person isn't wearing as much of an Ascendant costume as the rest of us, or the Ascendant costume is actually more reflective of this person's deeper self than is usually the case. Years ago, rather than dressing up at Halloween, one of my nieces wore a button that said, "This IS my costume."

Advantages? Life is simpler when the Sun's lessons and the Ascendant's lessons are the same. Since there's less experience of conflict between the style (Ascendant) and the ego (Sun), such a person can be very focused and direct. Disadvantages? Fewer places to hide; no Ascendant differences from the Sun can be used as cloaking devices for the Sun. Also, the Moon is the odd one out here. Therefore, such a person runs the risk of overidentifying with the attitudes and motivations of her Ascendant and her Sun, at the expense of her feelings and emotional needs (Moon). Unless she makes an effort to connect with her Moon, she runs the risk of being sane (Sun) and poised (Ascendant), but not very happy (Moon). She should be particularly careful not to project her inner life and emotional needs onto another person.

Imagine a woman with a first house Virgo Sun, Virgo rising and a Sagittarian Moon. Archetypally, our heroine is the Craftsperson or

Critic or Analyst or Perfectionist, wearing the mask of the Craftsperson or Critic or Analyst or Perfectionist. If she's developed some self-esteem and found the right work, she can be very centered and productive, and exude a lot of presence and natural authority (Sun). But what about her Sagittarian Moon's emotional needs for new experiences, for unstructured days full of adventure, variety and spontaneity? Unless our heroine has built time into her schedule to feed her Sagittarian heart, she may date a series of colorful, irrepressible, plucky men—who can turn out to be immature, irresponsible and scatterbrained Peter Pans. How to avoid this scenario? One way is to use her weekends and vacation time to satisfy her Moon. To go places she's never been, do things she's never done before, and take no work with her.

What if a man has the Moon conjunct the Ascendant, or the Moon in the first house and in the same sign as the Ascendant? Such a person must learn to wear his heart (Moon) on his sleeve (Ascendant), to act (Ascendant) *on* his feelings (Moon) without acting *out* his feelings. Regardless of this man's rising sign, his style should include the warmth, gentleness and soulfulness of the Moon. What's the downside? The first house is far from the preferred abode of the Moon. It can be timid, clannish, overly subjective and self-absorbed, and our culture tends to be less accepting of a yin lunar mask in a man than in a woman. Also, the Sun is the odd person out in this man's primal triad, so he runs the risk of being in touch with his feelings (Moon), and being poised (Ascendant), but operating with less ego strength and sanity (Sun) than he could. Is it good to act on your feelings *all* the time?

Say that a man has Libra rising, a first house Libra Moon and a Capricorn Sun. Archetypally, he is the Hermit, Executive, Prime Minister, Patriarch or Architect, with the heart of the Artist, Lover, Counselor and Diplomat, and the mask of the Artist, Lover, Counselor and Diplomat. Here, typically, would be someone with a good set of social skills, who is gentle, charming, aesthetically and interpersonally sensitive, and skilled at the fine art of compromise. Such a person has a profound desire for and thrives upon harmony and connection. Such a person also tends to be attractive to others: we all like to be both deeply and accurately *seen* (Libra) and nurtured (Moon).

So where's the downside? Our hero's Capricorn Sun must accomplish a Great Work or Works that are rooted in his own nature, regardless of the cost to his popularity or status. He can't let others' reactions deflect him from his chosen course, or his ego strength (Capricorn Sun) will be weakened. What does he do? I have an image of this man, working under a deadline (Capricorn Sun), successfully deflecting his fan club (Libra Moon and Ascendant) long enough to get to his office (Capricorn Sun), without hurting anybody's feelings. Perhaps he does what one writer I know once did: sends a letter to everyone he knows, explaining that he loves them all, but he must get this project finished by this date, so he won't be available socially or by telephone or email until after that date. And then he's throwing a party.

By now you'll have gathered that these conflicting Sun-Moon-Ascendant blends can be integrated, but that it takes conscious effort to do so. The Ascendant is, among other things, *partially a learned behavior.* Often such conscious effort happens only after a lot of unpleasant experiences which force us to recognize that something about our persona isn't working for us. If our Ascendant is the odd one out in the primal triad, we need to learn a way to wear that mask so that it doesn't pinch us. If the Sun or the Moon are the odd ones out, we need to learn not to let the Ascendant work overtime and take over their functions.

How do we learn this? I've offered some possible solutions in the examples above, but how might those people have arrived at those solutions?

Again, some answers may come from a place near the world of the theater, if not actually in it. They boil down to getting some awareness of how our Ascendant operates and of how others experience it. We might take a class that helps business people become more effective. We might join a Rotary Club and learn to make speeches, or have a friend video us at a party or as we give a lecture.

Last but not least, there's astrodrama. Find at least three astrologically-fluent friends. For our purposes here, I'd suggest you start with just the Sun, Moon and Ascendant, at least at first. One friend will play your Sun, one your Moon and one your Ascendant. The fourth, if you have a fourth, will take notes about their conversation.

Present your threefold "self" with a project or a quandary: asking someone for a date; asking the boss for a raise; deciding where to go on vacation; deciding where to move; deciding whether to have a child. The Sun person speaks for your Sun's agenda. The Moon person speaks for your Moon's needs and feelings. The Ascendant person participates in their dialog, sometimes mediating, and sometimes siding with or against the Sun or the Moon. When your threefold "self" reaches a consensus, the Ascendant person summarizes it for you, and can put an Ascendant-sign "spin" on that summary. Then the note-taker can fill you on how they reached that consensus.

Make this fun, but not a farce. If your friends know some astrology, know you well enough to get your number, and love you enough to be both *helpful* and *gentle,* I think you'll be amazed at the results. Then you can trade roles and perform someone else's Sun-Moon-Ascendant blend.

Do you have a lot of astrologically-fluent friends, enough to enlist six or more people? Steven and I taught an astrology class where we recruited two groups of six students each to play the Sun, the Moon, the Ascendant, Mercury, Venus and Mars in the charts of two six-part "people" who had to work out a conflict with one another. Once each six-part "person" had agreed on his or her position in that conflict, *only the Ascendant could talk to the other six-part "person's" Ascendant,* although each planet could keep commenting from "inside." Sometimes the Sun or the Moon or Mars got very rowdy about wanting the Ascendant to express that planet's views to the other "person!" If you find this type of scenario appealing, Barbara Schermer's *Astrology Alive* is a great book about astrodrama, with lots of suggestions for enacting an entire chart.

Besides the exercise above, some discussion points follow for those who want further exploration of the material in this chapter. The first four items will work best if you have access to lots of birth charts of people you know or have at least met, or if you own the Astrodatabank computer program.

1. Put all the charts with Aries Suns together. Then subdivide them by their Ascendants: all the Aries Suns with Aries rising, all the Aries Suns with Taurus rising, etc. Now think: in your experience of each person, how easy is it for him or her to express his or her Ascendant? Do you notice any patterns, such as an Aries Sun with a Fire sign rising seems more comfortable with its Ascendant than does an Aries Sun with a Water sign rising? Repeat this exercise for all the Sun signs in your collection of charts.

2. If you have enough charts, divide them into Sun-and-Moon piles: all the Aries Suns with Aries Moons, all the Aries Suns with Taurus Moons, etc. Then make a subdivision of those Sun-and-Moon piles by Ascendant: all the Aries Suns and Moons with Aries rising; all the Aries Suns and Moons with Taurus rising, etc. Ask yourself the same questions about these people that you asked in exercise number one. How does including the Moon in the blend refine your perceptions of these people?

3. Divide the charts into twelve piles by their Ascendant signs. Next, divide each Ascendant group into two piles: those who express that Ascendant easily, and those who don't. Follow your first instinct about who's expressing their Ascendants easily or not; don't stop too

long to ponder. Now pick up each chart and study it. Is there something in each particular Sun-Moon-Ascendant blend that might have tipped you off about whether it would be easy or difficult for that person to express that Ascendant? If you've known any of these people a long time, how have their expressions of their Ascendants changed over time?

4. Go through the charts and select everyone with the Sun and the Ascendant in the same sign, then everyone with the Moon and the Ascendant in the same sign. Think carefully about how that particular Sun or Moon shows up in that person's outer style.

5. If you don't have enough astrologically-savvy friends to help you enact your own Sun-Moon-Ascendant blend, then write down your Sun, Moon and Ascendant's three-way dialog about a real or imaginary conflict of yours. Who allies with whom? Who resists whom? If they all get along famously with one another, then how do they react when somebody else disagrees?

6. Rent a few movies and decide what Sun-Moon-Ascendant blends the leading characters have, or analyze some characters in a few novels. If you have astro-buddies who can assess the same characters, discuss your reasons for your conclusions, using evidence from the books or movies to support your views. For example, I think that Flora, the female lead in the delightful movie *Cold Comfort Farm,* is a Capricorn with a Cancer or perhaps a Virgo Moon, and Libra rising . . .

CHAPTER SIX: THE RULER OF THE ASCENDANT

Are you new to astrology, or could you use a refresher about which planets rule which signs? Here's a quick reference table:

Aries is ruled by **Mars**
Taurus is ruled by **Venus**
Gemini is ruled by **Mercury**
Cancer is ruled by **the Moon**
Leo is ruled by **the Sun**
Virgo is ruled by **Mercury**
Libra is ruled by **Venus**
Scorpio is co-ruled by **Pluto and Mars**
Sagittarius is ruled by **Jupiter**
Capricorn is ruled by **Saturn**
Aquarius is co-ruled by **Uranus and Saturn**
Pisces is co-ruled by **Neptune and Jupiter**

The planet ruling the sign of the Ascendant has been called, in some astrological circles, "the Lord of the chart." We don't need to think in quite such hierarchical terms, yet the ruler of the Ascendant and its house position are definitely of vital importance, both to the health of the Ascendant and that of the chart as a whole. In fact, the ruler of the Ascendant, its house position and its aspects rank in interpretive importance right after the Sun, Moon, Ascendant and lunar Nodes themselves.

Rectifying birth charts has repeatedly demonstrated the importance of the Ascendant's ruler to me. Rectification is a process by which an astrologer attempts to determine an accurate birth time. It's best done within a relatively narrow time frame; for example, when a client has objective reasons to state that she was born between noon and 4:00 p.m., rather than having no idea at all what time she was born, or merely intuiting her birth time. Once that time frame is objectively established, I ask the client to list the dates of two or three dozen very important events in her life, as accurately as she can remember them. Then I look at the transits and progressions on those important events to a series of possible birth charts whose birth times are evenly spaced between noon and 4:00 p.m.

When I'm determining whether the client has, say, Sagittarius or Capricorn rising, I've learned to look carefully at the client's Jupiter, which rules Sagittarius, and at the client's Saturn, which rules Capricorn. Whichever of those two planets is more involved, by transit or progression, with that client's list of important events is almost always the ruler of that client's Ascendant.

Remember that the Ascendant is in charge of "foreign relations." Think of the planet ruling the Ascendant as an ambassador from the Ascendant to the rest of the chart. Think of the house containing the ruler of the Ascendant as the country that the ambassador is visiting. That host country—the house containing the Ascendant's ruler—must treat that ambassador well, honoring it, letting it flourish, and giving it a certain measure of power. In return, a well-treated ambassador sends good energy back to the home country of the Ascendant, which is strengthened and made healthier and better-integrated.

The corollaries to that principle are also true: one, if you're making a less than optimal response to your Ascendant, then the house containing the Ascendant's ruler can be weakened; and two, if you're making a less than optimal response to the ruler of your Ascendant or to the house containing it, then your Ascendant itself can be weakened.

If you're having trouble understanding your Ascendant or getting it to function as well as you wish it did, then don't stop with merely working on your Ascendant itself. Make sure you're *also* working on the development of your Ascendant's ruling planet, its house position and aspects. Helping the *ambassador* (the ruler of your Ascendant), its *host country* (the house containing the ruler of your Ascendant) and any *allies* it may have (any planets aspecting the ruler of the

Ascendant) will help that ambassador's *home country*, the Ascendant itself.

What if your Ascendant has two planetary rulers? (See the table at the beginning of this chapter.) The same logic applies to both rulers. You have two ambassadors out there in their respective host countries. They both need to be well-treated in order to send good energy back to the home country, the Ascendant.

Ready for an example? Jennifer is a double sixth house Virgo with Aries rising. She's the Craftsperson or Analyst or Critic or Worker or Servant, with the heart (Moon) of the Craftsperson or Analyst or Critic or Worker or Servant. Jennifer's Virgo Sun and Moon and their sixth house placements all emphasize the importance of her finding the right work that lets her express herself in a personally meaningful way, helps her keep growing, and makes her feel whole. Not perfect, *whole*. Whole, as in fulfilled. Complete unto herself. Not lacking or less than, in any fundamental way. At the appropriate ages and stages of her work, it would be wise for Jennifer to seek good mentors in her chosen craft, and later to become such a mentor herself. Humility, willingness to engage in honest self-appraisal, and dedication to improvement are all important strategies for Jennifer.

With Aries rising, Jennifer's wearing the mask of the Warrior, the Survivor, the Daredevil, the Pioneer or the Heroine. How comfortably do you think the "fit" of Jennifer's Warrior's mask with the rest of her chart feels to her? What is a Craftsperson doing carrying weapons? How comfortable are the Servant or the Analyst with being armed to the teeth?

There's a certain silliness to those questions and images, but they help us start to think about Jennifer's Sun-Moon-Ascendant blend. A sixth house double Virgo is not automatically at ease with an Aries Ascendant, nor is an Aries Ascendant naturally skilled at handling foreign relations for a sixth house Virgo Sun and Moon.

But Jennifer needs to develop an assertive and confident (Aries) style (Ascendant). She will not be able to make full use of this incarnation—we incarnate *in a physical body*, and the Ascendant is the part of the chart that is most representative of the physical body—without learning how to use her Aries Ascendant well. It may help her set limits with The Boss or Mentor or Apprentice from Hell. It may help give her courage to pursue the right work. It may help her feel better if she's having adventures, so that her life doesn't deteriorate into nothing but work. Therefore, regardless of how awkwardly that Aries Ascendant fits with the rest of her chart, Jennifer has to learn to use it. If she finds it hard to "work" that Aries Ascendant directly—by taking assertiveness training classes or an Outward Bound course, perhaps—*then she could also approach the development of her Ascendant by working on a healthy expression of its ruling planet, Mars, wherever it lies in her house structure.*

If Jennifer has Mars in the first house, a double dose of experiences like those assertiveness training classes or Outward Bound expeditions we just mentioned are indicated all over again. However, if she *overdoes* her Ascendant, rather than underdoing it, we might add anger management classes to our list.

Let's take Mars briefly through the rest of Jennifer's houses.

Mars in the second house: In order to have healthy self-esteem, Jennifer needs Mars experiences (adventures and assertiveness and, probably, physical exercise: Mars needs to move). Also, Jennifer must take pro-active control of her financial life (second house). The wimpier she feels, the less she'll like herself, and the narrower the opportunity space she'll allow herself.

Mars in the third house: Jennifer needs to be good at asserting herself and defending herself with words, and she benefits from developing an active, dynamic, punchy style of communication, and from claiming her right to an interesting life, not just a busy one. If she fails in these tasks, she could be stressed out from sheer cognitive overload.

Mars in the fourth house: Jennifer needs to be careful not to let a parent with a strong personality dominate her; she must be able to set healthy boundaries in her family life. Also, she must be able to defend her home environment, and to claim a home and home life that work for her, lest they become a chronic battlefield.

Mars in the fifth house: A creative outlet is good for Jennifer, particularly one that involves performance. She needs to defend her right to have some recreational, unstructured time. She should set boundaries very early in a new relationship or friendship, or she could find herself bullied.

Mars in the sixth house: Developing the right craft will require a certain amount of sheer courage. Jennifer must be careful not to let overwork wear her down—the ability to say "no," and to claim what she wants at work, is essential to both her job satisfaction and her health. Otherwise, she could find herself the target of the office bullies.

Mars in the seventh house: Jennifer benefits immensely from relationships with spunky, direct, energetic people—and if she doesn't develop enough assertiveness to keep from being bulldozed by them, she's headed for trouble and stress in her relating life.

Mars in the eighth house: Jennifer's natural mate, and the friends who'll make the deepest psychological impact upon her, are towers of strength. That profound level of eighth-house intimacy spooks her. And it should, if she's not strong enough herself to "tell the truth and shame the devil."

Mars in the ninth house: The philosophy of life that works best for Jennifer could be summarized as "Feel the fear, and do it anyway." A life whose major decisions are based on fear is no life at all for her. She may need to insist on her right to follow this particular vibrant star, or find herself bored half to death.

Mars in the tenth house: As her "cosmic job description," Jennifer should symbolize courage and energy, or adventurousness, or even heroism to her community. If she's not brave enough to claim that role, a less healthy one is possible: that of victim.

Mars in the eleventh house: To accomplish goals that are truly meaningful to her, Jennifer needs "troops": feisty live wires who aren't afraid to make noise and take up space. A healthy response here means that Jennifer will get pluckier with age, while a less than optimal response may leave her a stressed and contentious little old lady.

Mars in the twelfth house: Jennifer's inner guru is a mystical warrior. The right use of courage and willpower can be a profound aid in the development of her spiritual life. On the other hand, she could be spurred toward spiritual growth by losing her temper in embarrassing ways. The choice is hers . . .

Here are some exercises for astrologers or students who want further exploration of the material in this chapter:

1. Take the charts of two or three dozen people you know well, who seem to have reasonably happy lives, and whom you've known long enough to have observed them in more than one context. (In other words, if you met them at work, you've also spent time with them outside the office.) Divide the charts into twelve piles: Ascendant ruler in the first house, in the second house, in the third house, etc. Think carefully about how and where you experience that Ascendant ruler's behavior in that person's life.

2. Now look at the charts of six or eight frustrated or unhappy people whom you know well, and whom you know in more than one context (e.g., not just at work). Where are the rulers of their Ascendants? Chances are that those houses aren't working very well for those people. What behavior do you think they might need to change in those houses in order to be less frustrated? (Please remember that this is just a study tool—it's best not to offer advice when no one's asked you for it.)

3. Go back to your chart files and pick out everyone with the same sign rising. Now make twelve piles from each rising sign: Ascendant ruler in the first, in the second, in the third, etc. How do you

experience people who have Leo rising and an eighth house Sun, compared to people with Leo rising and a second house Sun?

4. Consider the house containing the ruler of your own Ascendant. How much time do you spend there? How many of your activities revolve around that house? What's working for you there? What would you like to change? If you enjoy and are comfortable working with active imagination, try opening a dialog with the ruler of your Ascendant. (Robert Johnson's book *Inner Work* is an excellent place to start learning about active imagination.) What is the ruling planet's name? What is it wearing? What are its tools? What kind of house does it live in? Does it have any company there (any other planets)? With whom is it in regular dialogue (what planets does it aspect)? Ask it what it needs from you, and if there's anything it would like to tell you. (You don't have to agree!)

5. Try a thought experiment: imagine that the ruler of your Ascendant had been in a different house. What would it feel like to have that house more emphasized in your life? How might your behavior and schedule differ from what they are now? Repeat the experiment for all of the houses.

If this exercise is hard to think about, try it this way: imagine you're the U.S. ambassador to France. If you don't do a good job there, World War Three may not be declared, but the political, economic and cultural relationships between the two countries will suffer, creating needless tension and instability. How do you need to behave to get along with the French? Now imagine you're the U.S. ambassador to Australia. Then imagine you're the U.S. ambassador to Spain, then Japan, then Germany. You're still you in each of those countries, but when your environment and its customs and agendas differ, your behavior needs to differ in response to them.

CHAPTER SEVEN:
TRANSITS, PROGRESSIONS, ARCS AND THE ASCENDANT

With a transit, progression or arc that is aspecting the natal Ascendant, it's as if *another being* (the transiting, progressing or arcing planet) is either *visiting your Ascendant directly* (the conjunction), or *communicating with it* (the other aspects) from another house (the house containing the transiting, progressing or arcing planet).

Do you *like* that entity's visit or communication? The answer to that question depends on two factors. One factor is how comfortable you are with that visiting or communicating planet in the first place. A triple Libra typically isn't thrilled about astrological events involving Mars, but is much more open to those of Venus. The second factor is the nature of the aspect that planet is making. We tend to feel more at ease with a planetary visitor or communication if the aspect it makes is a trine or a sextile, and less at ease if it's a square or an opposition. Conjunctions can go either way, depending, again, on how comfortable we are with that planet in the first place.

The "visiting entity" metaphor works well for all transits, progressions and arcs *to* the natal Ascendant. With progressions or arcs *of* the natal Ascendant, your *style and mask* need to evolve and change. It's as if you are shedding your skin and growing another skin.

If your progressed or arced Ascendant is *aspecting the natal Ascendant,* how comfortable you are with your Ascendant's change is indicated partly by whether the aspect it makes is flowing (trines and sextiles) or tense (squares and oppositions—conjunctions can go either way). If your progressed or arced Ascendant is *moving into another sign or house*, how comfortable you are with that change is indicated by how comfortable you are with that sign or house.

If the progressed or arced Ascendant is aspecting one of your natal planets, then part of that metamorphosis also involves a *dialog* with that natal planetary being. Whether that dialog resembles an agreement or an argument is indicated by whether the aspect is flowing or tense.

In any case—transits, or progressions and arcs, which are a kind of progression—the Ascendant needs to learn something, to incorporate the message or lesson of the transit, progression or arc. A general rule of thumb is that if you have been *overdoing* some quality of your Ascendant, it's time to *soften* that quality, according to the input of the transit, progression or arc. On the other hand, if you have been *underdoing* some quality of the Ascendant, it's time to *step up* the expression of that quality, according to the input of the transit, progression or arc.

Before we consider a few examples, some other theoretical points should addressed. While transits, progressions or arcs involving the Ascendant always say something about the ongoing development of your Ascendant in the sense of your *style or persona* (in the colloquial rather than in the Jungian sense of that word), they may also show up in your outer life. They may affect your *body*, since the Ascendant is so connected to the body. They may be felt in your *relationships,* since the Ascendant opposes the Descendant, which is the cusp of the house of relationships.

To some extent, of course, those points apply to any transit, progression or arc *to* or *of* any part of the birth chart. All astrological events signal a need for inner growth, transformation, and learning, and for the integration of those lessons. All astrological events may also be felt in your outer, biographical or even physical life.

As a general rule of thumb, the less able or willing you are to do the inner work around an astrological event, the more that astrological event will tend to express itself in your outer life. Why? Because it's in the nature of energy to manifest, to do something, to work. Astrological energies have to go *somewhere* and do *something*. Someone with very little inner life, or very little awareness of an inner life, leaves the astrological energy little if any place to work but in his or her outer life.

Astrologer Liz Greene has theorized that before we became aware of the human unconscious, we tended to experience astrological events more in our outer lives than on an inner level. Suppose that Saturn transited your fourth house cusp two or three hundred years ago. During that era, you were more likely to have your landlord throw you out for not paying the rent, and to wind up begging on the streets or living in the poorhouse, than you were to uncover during psychotherapy how much your cold, domineering or withdrawn father's influence affected your personal life and job choices.

I'm positive that Greene's theory is correct. Unfortunately, while we can sometimes study the biographies of people who lived two or three hundred years ago, we can't go back in time and interview them. Yet, at the risk of sounding silly, I have a way that I can sort of observe this theory at work. You might have such a way yourself. I live with two beings who don't have much of an inner life as we understand that term and who have, as far we know, no knowledge of their unconscious minds. Since I have their birth charts, I have front row seats on how their transits and progressions unfold in their outer lives. I'm talking about my cats. Bear with me, please; I have no intention of becoming an animal astrologer, and I promise that this will be interesting as well as entertaining.

As transiting Saturn approached the Aquarian Ascendant of our late and much-missed cat, Pyanfar, Steven and I joked about what Great Work she would have to undertake (Saturn), and how she would have to mature and become more responsible (Saturn), and to insist on her right to be taken more seriously as she assumed more outward *gravitas* (Saturn on the Ascendant). Neither one of us took this dialog seriously—until Pyanfar developed a painful case of cystitis. At that point we started to pay attention, because Saturn traditionally rules crystallization, and feline cystitis involves the formation of crystals in the urine.

Another of our cats came from a home where someone had abused her. She escaped that environment by moving to our house with Mars transiting over her Sagittarian fourth house cusp and squaring her Virgo Ascendant. It was stressful (Mars) for her to leave the fourth house "land of her birth," but a good move for her, since that land was dangerous (Mars). A Cancer Sun and still a kitten at the time, she hid under our bed for several days, until she worked up the courage (Mars) for brief ventures out to inspect her new digs (fourth house). A few days later, she celebrated her improved circumstances by an impromptu (transiting Mars in Sagittarius) and unhygienic (squaring her Virgo Ascendant) sprint through Steven's just-prepared dinner plate, as if she were saying, "I'm safe here! Whee!"

Guess what happened several years later when transiting Uranus moved into the orbs of a conjunction to this cat's Piscean seventh house cusp? A sudden and unexpected Uranus-in-Pisces lightning bolt struck in her relationship life (seventh house), in the person of our affectionate, exuberant and unbelievably klutzy new kitten, Clouseau. Clouseau spent months on end ambushing (Uranus) the older cat, invading her personal space and leaping on her (Uranus opposing her Ascendant) at every possible opportunity, mostly on purpose, sometimes by glorious accident. The kitten just wanted to play, but the poor cat was so traumatized and jumpy that it took a long time and extra attention not only for her to accept Clouseau (seventh house), but to repair her relationship with Steven and me.

Back to Pyanfar. When Jupiter transited over her Leo seventh house cusp, we joked about that too. Py was already so pampered; how could her seventh house get any better? Lo and behold, a fat, friendly, lordly orange tomcat (Jupiter in Leo) showed up at our door and fell in love with her (seventh house). Py was neutered, and she usually repelled feline trespassers in the spirit of her third house Aries Sun: ferociously and at ear-splitting volume. But she fell right back in love with this orange tom. They played chase in our yard. They sunned themselves side by side on our deck. They followed each other in and out of our treehouse. Py was confused when he made physical advances—Jupiter was *opposing* her Ascendant—but to our astonishment she didn't try to kill him, and they were still inseparable. As Jupiter left the orbs of the aspect, the tom disappeared; perhaps his owners moved.

I've told you these cat stories for more than your amusement: to illustrate how, when someone has little inner life as a psychologist would understand that term, an astrological event can show up in his or her *outer* life in some concrete, biographical, physical or otherwise externally-oriented way. Such outward manifestations are all well and good for our pets, but we humans need to be careful not to let the astrological events that affect us show up *only in our outer lives*. If human beings do that, they are probably being reactive, not pro-active. They are not consciously participating in their own growth as fully as they might.

Because the Ascendant is in charge of foreign relations, astrological events involving the Ascendant are ones that we may be particularly prone to channel into our outer circumstances without doing any inner work. *However, events involving the Ascendant frequently need both an inner and an outer response, because of the inner and outer nature of the Ascendant itself.*

For example, if Uranus transits over your Ascendant, and the one response you make is to shave your head and dye your scalp electric blue, you'd better look carefully at yourself and at your life. Why? Because there's very likely to be some other and far more important War of Independence (Uranus) that you are not fighting. In fact, you may be avoiding that work of self-examination and individuation by trying to aim the transit only and entirely at your outer life, in this case at your appearance.

What if you aim the transit only or mostly at your inner life? Is that even possible? Yes, it is. I have a client who, during a Venusian event involving the Ascendant, kept a lengthy and detailed journal about a totally imaginary relationship with a media personality. My client was single, wasn't doing anything creative when the Venusian event began, and hadn't dated anyone in a long time. All of that changed, partly, we both think, because when the client realized how that Venusian energy was all being channeled, albeit creatively, into an *imaginary* relationship, the journal's details could then be analyzed in the light of what sort of *real relationship and creative outlets* my client might want. The journal was a safe way to practice the Venus-work on an inner level, before taking the work into the outside world. As my client became more outgoing, affable and accessible, and let other people see and enjoy some of that vivid imagination, she started enjoying both an improved relating life and a previously unexplored art form.

Ready for some more examples?

Janine is a tenth house Pisces with Gemini rising and a twelfth house Taurus Moon. Despite that Gemini Ascendant, linear communication has not been her strong suit—much of what an earthy Taurus Moon feels or senses can be hard to articulate in words, while a Pisces Sun can be prone to perceptions that don't entirely mesh with three-dimensional consensus reality.

Along comes Saturn transiting over Janine's Gemini Ascendant. She has been *underdoing* the mask of the Perceiver, Communicator, Observer, Witness or Storyteller—her Gemini persona. Janine is an independent film maker, with a knack for highly evocative images. Her work is prime art house material, if only it could get funding and distribution. How could that happen? This sounds like a job for practical Saturn's transit over her Gemini Ascendant. Imagine that Saturn is an entity, a being, who's come to visit Janine's Ascendant. What sort of being? A Wise Elder. An efficiency expert. A master strategist. An organized executive. In their highest expressions, all of these beings operate with absolute integrity (Saturn), and help Janine accomplish some Great Work (Saturn), by helping her face reality (Saturn) and adjust her behavior and outer self (Ascendant) according to the demands of that Great Work.

The reality (Saturn) is that if Janine can't put herself forward (Ascendant) and effectively (Saturn) communicate (Gemini) her need for funding and distribution, her work won't get the recognition it deserves. The late astrologer Grant Lewi, writing in the 1930s and 1940s, called Saturn "the cosmic paycheck"—we get what we deserve during Saturnian events. I would add that we get what we deserve *if* we work for it in a logical, efficient, realistic, mature, responsible and competent Saturnian manner.

Janine has some Saturn homework to do. What might transiting Saturn tell her? "Go to a library (Gemini Ascendant). Research (Gemini) grants and awards and funding available to film makers. Ask the right (Saturn) questions (Gemini). Find the *facts* (Saturn and Gemini) about funding and distribution, rather than stay mired in wishful thinking. And don't remain tongue-tied (insufficiently utilized Gemini Ascendant). Maybe that will involve some coaching (Saturn) about how to be an effective communicator (Gemini Ascendant)."

Yes, this is hard work (Saturn) for Janine. But without it, she'll be short-changing herself and her art.

What if Janine were overdoing her Gemini Ascendant instead? What might that behavior look like? Running around in circles, being overextended, chattering her head off, phones ringing constantly, no organization, no goals, no strategy, just frenzied busy-ness. In this case, transiting Saturn might counsel her, "Slow down and get organized. Turn on your answering machine. Clear out your clutter. Set your priorities carefully. Communicate strategically, not indiscriminately—save your breath and conserve your energy. What's the most important thing you have to do to get funding? And the next most important thing? And the next? What can you delegate? If you need help figuring that out, ask the three most efficient people you know."

Let's stay with Janine's chart and look at some more astrological events. Her progressed Sun, now in Aries and the eleventh house, is sextiling her Gemini Ascendant. Her natal mask of the Observer (Gemini Ascendant) needs to integrate the energy of her evolving ego (progressed Sun), which is learning about courage, drive and setting limits (Aries), in order to accomplish goals that are meaningful to her (eleventh house). In turn, Janine's evolving ego (progressed Sun) needs a communicative, articulate, curious, open-minded (Gemini) style (Ascendant) in order to become braver and more feisty (progressed Sun in Aries), and to claim a future (eleventh house) that works for her.

What might the communication (sextile) between Janine's progressed Sun and natal Gemini Ascendant sound like? The progressed eleventh house Aries Sun might say, "I need adventures. I need to develop my will. I need to test myself (Aries). Sometimes I'm scared to do that (Aries), but if I don't, I won't have an exciting (Aries) future (eleventh house); I'll have a stressful one (lower level response to Aries)."

The natal Gemini Ascendant might say, "That sounds good to me (sextile), because I need to get better at juggling data and experiences and ideas (Gemini) in order to make sure that my life stays interesting (Gemini). I need to walk my talk (Ascendant); I need to put my money where my mouth is (Ascendant). I could use some extra energy (Sun) to help me do that. I have to persuade people to fund my projects, and having some more magnetism and charisma (Sun) would help me win them over."

Meanwhile, Janine's Ascendant is progressing into Leo. Her evolving style (progressed Ascendant) needs to develop some Leonine characteristics. She needs to put on a Leo-skin (progressed Ascendant), to augment and assist her natal Gemini-skin. Think of Leo costumes being added to that Gemini wardrobe. Janine needs to present herself (Ascendant) with more color, confidence and flair (Leo). She needs to make more of an impact (Leo). She needs to radiate the energy of the Performer, Queen or Aristocrat. We're talking about the good Queen and the benevolent Aristocrat, for whom *noblesse oblige*—not the tyrant or the snob. We're talking about the sunny, endearing Performer, not the prima donna.

Janine's progressed Ascendant is also squaring her natal fifth house Neptune in Scorpio. A dialog is in progress between her new Leo-skin (progressed Ascendant) and her natal Neptune and, since the aspect is a square, the dialog starts out as a disagreement. Neptune might say, "Why are you being so noisy all of a sudden (progressed Ascendant in Leo)? Don't you know I need peace and quiet and free-floating, non-linear time (Neptune) in order for my creative juices to flow (fifth house)?" The progressed Ascendant might answer, "That's not all you need any more. If we want anyone else to appreciate what those creative juices have produced, we'll have to call attention to ourselves. Would anyone bother to watch a two hour documentary of someone just sitting there meditating with his eyes closed? Well, no one's going to notice our work if we just sit there and imagine stuff all by ourselves. If we want an audience, we need to get *interesting!* We need *advertising!*"

We could go on describing that dialog, but its goal is to reach an agreement between the progressed Ascendant in Leo and the natal fifth house Neptune *that meets some of the needs of each configuration.* Because the progressed aspect between them is a square, they both have to win partially and lose partially. Janine still gets non-linear quiet time to feed her creativity, and she also learns to communicate more engagingly about that creative work, in order to draw in her prospective audience. A good compromise would be communicating in a whimsical Neptunian way as well as in a colorful Leonine way.

Some exercises follow for those who want further exploration of the material in this chapter:

1. Look at the current or past transits affecting your own Ascendant. Imagine what planetary beings (transiting planets) are or were involved. Give them costumes, props, agendas and names that fit the signs and houses they occupy. (For example, a planet in Aries might be wearing a uniform; a planet in Libra might be carrying a cosmetic case or a set of paints; a planet in Scorpio might want to

psychoanalyze the Ascendant or perform an exorcism upon it, etc.) Write a script of the dialogs that might occur. What does each transiting planet want your Ascendant *to learn (inner level)* and *to do (outer level)?*

2. Apply exercise one to the chart of a famous person or to that of a client.

3. Apply exercises one and two using the current or past progressions or arcs of planets affecting your natal Ascendant.

4. Consider the current or past progressions of your Ascendant. If it changed signs, what costumes need to be added to your Ascendant's wardrobe? Did you experience any such shift on a literal level or on an energetic level, or both?

5. Consider the current or past progressions of your Ascendant. If it aspected a natal planet, what sort of dialog occurred? How did you feel about it?

6. Apply exercises four and five to the chart of a famous person or to that of a client.

7. If you have some astro-buddies with a silly streak, try throwing a small party where everyone comes dressed as an astrological energy (or even carrying one prop that describes that astrological energy) that is currently affecting his or her Ascendant. Everyone should be prepared to describe the dialog that his or her Ascendant might be engaged in with another planet, if such an aspect is happening. If transiting Neptune is making an aspect to your Ascendant, for example, you might bring a crystal ball. If the aspect is a square or an opposition, you're having an argument about using that crystal ball. Swap charts and discuss one another's astrological events. Keep it light, keep it moving and have fun with it. (Think of all the stories you can take away for illustrations in your readings!)

8. If no one wants to dress up or bring props for exercise seven, then make it a purely verbal exercise. Just describe what you would have worn or brought if you had all done so, and what the dialogues might be.

9. Get a copy of Barbara Schermer's book *Astrology Alive*, and try an evening or evenings of astrodrama based on the astrological events affecting your Ascendants.

CHAPTER EIGHT: "ADJUSTING" YOUR ASCENDANT

Can the leopard change its spots?

Good question.

I hesitated to include this chapter, because there is a difference between *our behavior and our outer selves (Ascendant)*, and *our essential natures*. Some traits in our natures are probably not changeable, but how we cope with a characteristic, display it, conceal it or compensate for it can all be adjusted. Other traits can grow and shift a bit, and still others can change a lot. It can take a while to figure out which characteristics are which. If you're ever in doubt on that score, allow yourself plenty of time for reflection.

When you think about "adjusting" your Ascendant, think about changing your *behavior*—not your essence. It's important not to let others shame or criticize you for your essential nature. For example, if you have prominent Scorpio, Pluto or eighth house energies, and someone tells you that you're too intense, you might smile, agree that you do have a lot of intensity, and change the subject as soon as you politely can. Telling someone not to be intense is like telling him to change his blood type. But if someone respectfully suggests that you could have handled *a specific situation* differently, because *how you expressed* your intensity in that instance was counterproductive, you might do well to listen carefully and even ask for pointers, because that person is talking about your behavior, not your essence.

The Ascendant is among the astrological configurations that are most able to be consciously changed or adjusted or transformed. Not entirely—someone with Cancer rising will seldom be a flaming extravert, and few shrinking violets are numbered among Sagittarian Ascendants. But since the Ascendant is in many ways learned behavior, within the range of possibilities and the archetypal field or fields represented by its sign and any planets it contains, we can also learn to exhibit behavior from elsewhere within that range. Cancer rising, the mask of the Invisible Person, the hermit crab in its shell, may not *be* extraverted, but it can learn to *act* in a warm manner—because among the other faces of Cancer are the Healer or the Nurturer.

Say that you're having a transit or progression involving your Ascendant, and you've decided it's time for your mask to grow. Time to make some changes. Time for your outer self (Ascendant) to do a better job reflecting the person you are today. Or perhaps you need to adjust your Ascendant for one difficult afternoon, rather than aim for more lasting changes. (Someone once offered to loan me his Aries Ascendant for a day.) In either case, how can you make such changes?

It's hard to push the river, and growth has its own pace. But you can certainly think about growth while it's happening. You can at least attempt to cooperate with the growth process by how you behave.

For the purposes of this chapter, let's consider some material in the exercises that conclude our other chapters. I suggest you take the time to review the exercises:

* from Chapter Three, "Acting and the Ascendant;"
* from Chapter Four, "The Ascendant with the Sun and the Moon;"
* from Chapter Six, "The Ruler of the Ascendant;"
* and from Chapter Seven, "Transits, Progressions, Arcs and the Ascendant."

I'll try not to repeat material here that I've already covered on those pages. The end of this chapter won't have any separate exercises, because they're included in the remainder of the chapter itself.

Remember our discussion of how incongruent behavior makes a character seem suspicious and untrustworthy? Think about the change or changes you want to make, and how your behavior can stay congruent with those changes. If you want to become a more tolerant person, for example, don't hang onto the body language of a rigid one. Uncross your arms. Stop scowling. Lower your voice. Don't glance meaningfully at your watch if someone's only two minutes late.

Good salespeople, effective psychotherapists, inspiring ministers and persuasive politicians all know a lot about how to "tweak" their Ascendants. They need such skills in order to establish rapport with their clients, parishioners or voters. Talk to any friends you have in sales, counseling, the ministry or politics, and ask what skills allow them to connect with people. Be specific. If you're trying to develop a more confident persona, for example, ask how your friends convey confidence, so you'll have some idea what mannerisms you might think about developing. Ask what behaviors or gestures convey a lack of confidence, too, so you'll get a sense of what you might need to avoid doing. Your friends may not always know the answers to your questions, or their methods of establishing rapport may be automatic and semi-unconscious. Still, their answers may help you stay congruent.

Other types of people have skills in tweaking their Ascendants—con artists, babe magnets and femme fatales. I hope you don't know *too* many of the first sort, but if you do, spend some time observing them, as well as observing the latter two types. How do these people make a connection? Exude charm? Win trust? Watch the movie *Catch Me If You Can*, where Leonardo di Caprio plays a successful con artist. How does his character convince people that he's on the level? For a farce along the same lines, try *Dirty Rotten Scoundrels*, and watch Michael Caine. Why is his character more convincing than the novice grifter played by Steve Martin?

Talk to your friends or colleagues who are *gentle, supportive, perceptive and honest,* and who come across that way, too. All four traits are important here, and remember we're talking about behavior as well as essence. Ask such friends which of your behaviors when you first meet people might need changing, in order for you to give a first impression other than the one you're giving now. Is your initial presentation of yourself too timid? Too brash? Too scattered? If you have no idea how to make those changes, remember to consider the house that contains the ruler of your Ascendant. If you can adjust your behavior in that house, it can help you adjust your Ascendant, too.

Consider any dreams you may have about clothing. They can sometimes be valuable messages from your deep Self about your Ascendant. You can learn to remember your dreams. Keep pencil, paper and a flashlight by your bed. Tell yourself, before you go to sleep, that you'll remember what you dream. If you wake up in the night, turn on the flashlight and write down any fragments of any dreams. (I suggest a flashlight because it's easier than turning on your bedside lamp, and less likely to prevent your falling back asleep after you've made the notes.) Write down any dream recall first thing in the morning, because it will fade later in the day. If you are patient and persistent, you'll eventually start remembering some dreams. Watch them for clues about how your current expression of your Ascendant might or might not be working for you. For example, if you dream that you're embarrassed to find yourself naked, your Ascendant's protective function may need to be turned up. If you dream that you're wearing clothes that are too tight for you, your Ascendant may be too restrictive and not expressive enough. If you dream that someone else is forcing you to wear something, that person may be having too great an impact on your Ascendant. If you dream that some benevolent person gives you a cloak of invisibility, you may need to use your Ascendant to guard your inner life more carefully.

This suggestion may sound ridiculous, but have some fun with wearing or using a piece of clothing or an accessory that symbolizes the change that you're trying to make in the expression of your Ascendant. Acquiring the clothing will help you set an intention and remain conscious of it. Need to act braver and more adventuresome?

Buy something red, or a pair of hiking boots. Need to be more gentle? Try something in a soft dove-grey fabric. Need to be taken more seriously by yourself and others? How about an appointment book, a DayTimer or a PDA? Are you stuck? Then ask your most playful friend to help you brainstorm about your "costume" or "prop." Are you on a tight budget? Then try Ebay or the local thrift shop.

Your body is what literally embodies your Ascendant and helps to transmit its energy. Do something non-punitive to help yourself inhabit your body more fully. You might try a stroll, a massage, yoga, Tai Chi, Rolfing, swimming, dance, or joining a gym—whatever helps you experience your entire "spaceship." But start gradually and take it easy. If you punish your body, you won't want to repeat the experience.

Use an astrological computer program to calculate what major transits, progressions or arcs have involved your Ascendant at various times in your life. Then find as many photos or videos of yourself as you can from those time periods. Clear off a table that you won't need for anything else for at least a few days, lay out the photos chronologically, and put a note by each one stating what astrological event was happening then. Study the photos and think about the astrological events. Write down anything that occurs to you about what you were feeling, what happened, how you behaved and how you might have behaved instead, but don't criticize yourself. This is a learning experiment, and if you punish yourself, you won't learn as much, nor will you be eager to repeat the experience.

If you have astro-buddies, share the experiment with them. Maybe they'll want to set up their own photos on their own tables. Leave the photos on the table as long as you can, and write down any new thoughts every couple of days. Finally, in the light of what you've learned, think about what transits, progressions or arcs are now or soon will be affecting your Ascendant.

Don't have an astrology computer program? Go to www.astro.com or www.astrology.com to cast charts online for free.

Above all, have fun with this process. Think creatively, and I bet you'll come up with other ways to "tweak" the expression of your Ascendant.

CHAPTER NINE:
THE ASCENDANT AND "NATIONAL CHARACTER"

We're on shaky ground when we talk about charts of entire nations. Charts of *governments* (republics, constitutions, etc.) are easy to cast, if we have the exact date, time and place that an official governing entity went into effect. But it's hard to determine the chart of *a whole people*, its national character, its typical mentality. Then why are we bothering to examine this concept? Because this sort of speculation can teach us a lot about that rising sign in general, as well as about that nation in particular.

I suspect that when we caricaturize or stereotype a nation and its people, we base that caricature largely upon something corresponding to that national character's *"Ascendant:"* the body language, outer behavior and usual manner of self-presentation of its people. Their customs. Their etiquette. How we might identify people as natives of that country if we saw them on the street. I surmise that sometimes a national character's Ascendant coincides with that country's current government's Ascendant, and that sometimes it doesn't. Also, it's doubtful that the national character of an entire people changes every time its government does.

Have some fun—gently, please—with this notion of the correlations between a people's or a nation's Ascendant and the stereotypes or typical culture mores of those people. Again, a people's "national character" may not have the same chart as its country's current government. I'll soon run out of countries with whom I have enough experience to speculate about their national characters' Ascendants, but here are some examples to get you started thinking along these lines.

There's an ongoing debate about the U.S.A.'s horoscope, particularly over whether it has Sagittarius or Gemini rising. I agree with the Sibly birth chart, which gives it Sagittarius rising, an eighth house Cancer Sun and a second house Aquarius Moon. (July 4, 1776,

5:10 p.m., Philadelphia, PA. For more versions of the U.S.A. chart, please go to http://www.astrodatabank.com/NM/USA.htm.)

As Liz Greene says, the rest of the world tends to view Americans in a Sagittarian light, not in a Geminian light. I think Greene is right. The world sees Americans as cowboys, adventurers, naïve enthusiasts, or fat-bellied Jupiter clones. Foreigners see us as either athletic (Sagittarius rising) or self-indulgent (someone with a strong Jupiter can love the good life, and Jupiter rules Sagittarius). Foreigners remark on Americans' religious fervor, our extraversion or simply our loudness (more faces of Sagittarius). They see a "typical" American far more as all of the above than they do as questioning, articulate, open-minded intellectuals (Gemini).

When I lived in France, I quickly learned to spot other Americans partly from their clothes (typically looser and more comfortable than those of the French) and their shoes (often walking shoes, hiking boots, etc.), and partly from their gait and their body language. Most Americans stride along as if we have the whole wild West still left to explore. We swing our arms; we take up space. We slouch in our chairs. We act casual. We tend to be extraverted and inquisitive. The French tend to stand erect and to hold their limbs closer to their bodies, and their gaits and posture are more dignified and less slapdash. The French have smaller "space bubbles" around their bodies, and are more careful about defending theirs and not trangressing upon yours. They're generally less likely to strike up conversations with strangers. When I asked French friends about French stereotypes of Americans, I usually heard something along the lines of "a loud, fat, self-important businessman or a rich oil man" or "a cowboy." Doesn't that sound like Sagittarius and Jupiter to you? These same French friends admired Americans' pluckiness and willingness to try new things—Sagittarius again.

When Steven and I traveled in Ireland, we were almost always mistaken for Canadians. It happened so often that we started to ask why. The Irish invariably did some polite prevaricating when we questioned them. The Irish are among the kindest, most helpful, compassionate, warm and generous-spirited people I've ever met. One hatless, coatless, umbrella-less man chased us a couple of blocks through the rain, just because he thought we *might* be lost. I haven't spent enough time in Ireland to analyze their national character, but my first guess would be that it's Piscean. The Irish almost always wound up saying they thought that Steven and I were Canadian because we were "soft-spoken"—not Sagittarian-loud.

When I asked Norwegian relatives visiting my family what most struck them about American culture and Americans, they exchanged glances and said, "All the things to make you comfortable. Cushions and labor-saving devices." Jupiter, again, with its sense of entitlement. (And if, as I speculate later, the Norwegian national character has Taurus rising, what would they most be likely to notice?)

Years ago, a delightful, funny and very kind Italian woman attended one of my French classes. One day we were giving her some good-natured teasing about the stereotype of the romantic Italian, and she was laughing right along with us. Then she said, more seriously, "I think Americans are *much* more romantic, because you are such idealists." Sagittarius, again.

I think the British national character has Capricorn rising, although its most accepted governmental chart, according to an astrologer friend in the U.K., has a Capricorn Sun with Libra rising. That chart's data is Jan. 1, 1801, 12:01 a.m., London, when the Great Britain-Ireland union occurred. My friend's source is the book *Mundane Astrology: An Introduction to the Astrology of Nations and Groups,* by Michael Baigent, Nicholas Campion and Charles Harvey. Three more British governmental charts are listed in Doris Chase Doane's *Accurate World Horoscopes,* and two of the three have Capricorn rising: the England-Scotland union (May 1, 1707, 12:00 a.m., London), and the Statute of Westminster (Dec. 12, 1931, 9:30 a.m., Westminster).

What are some of our clichés about the British? They are a nation of stiff upper lips—Capricorn's self-control. Everyone must be properly introduced: Capricorn's reserve. High tea—there's a Capricorn ritual. The importance of tradition; the old school tie; the emphasis on the royal family. The awareness of class structure—Capricorn is very aware of hierarchy and status. The long arm of the prim and proper Victorian era. Once upon a time, the sun never set on the British Empire. The crusty old colonel who lived in India is practically a Capricorn stock character. The classics. Foggy weather and harsh (Capricorn) winters have helped shape the British national character. Conservatism.

Don't forget the flip side of Capricorn: capriciousness. Once there's a crack in that controlled Capricorn façade, no one can write farcical, offbeat humor like the British. Often that humor mocks some stuffy Capricorn trait. Moreover, there's the Capricorn ability to think strategically. In my opinion, the British write the finest, most complex and compelling murder mysteries in print. While the Saturn-ruled may not be more musically talented than the rest of us, they can certainly exhibit more discipline about the practice necessary to excel at music, and the British have written some of the best (rock) music of our era, too.

How about the French national character? I've spent more time in France than in the U.K., so I can go into more detail here. My vote is for Leo rising, although Doane gives the birth data for its current form of government, the Fifth Republic, as Oct. 6, 1958, 6:21 p.m., Paris. That chart has a Libra Sun, a Cancer Moon, and Aries rising.

Here, I think the national character of this culture is at variance with the governmental chart. The Libran Sun is interesting, in that Libra was an early candidate for my choice of the French national character, but the French have an international reputation for sheer style and flair that's bigger than Libran elegance. If it's French, it must be cool; it must "rule" (Leo). That's more Leo than Libra. There is a *tremendous* French concern with appearances (Leo), including stylish or at least appropriate dress, and a lot of changing dos and don'ts about what appropriate dress is. It is not uncommon for the French to iron their T shirts. Think of Louis XIV, the "Sun King" (Leo), who made a whole autocratic political power ritual (Sun) out of which nobles were allowed to help him get dressed in the morning.

The French often appear haughty (Leo) to non-Francophiles. There's a distinctly French desire to maintain dignity, to save face, (Leo), a distaste for being or even appearing wrong. There's a desire to maintain their sovereignty (Leo), as individuals and as a nation. During the first Gulf War, France carefully "affirmed its solidarity at the same time as its independence." The French do not cooperate well in traffic, as if everyone's King in his own car and wants to be King of the road, too. Given how many strikes are happening at any given time, some Francophobes might say that the French don't cooperate well elsewhere, either.

There's a Leonine gallantry between the sexes in France. The French flirt exceptionally well—remember that Leo is the natural ruler of the fifth house. There's a respect for creativity, for intelligence, for anyone who "shines;" remember, the Sun is a star. There can be a "chacun pour soi," everyone-for-himself, Leonine sort of egotism, or even cults of personality—the covers of French CDs tend to have a large close-up of the musician, who looks majestic and intense. Break through that regal demeanor the right way, however, with plenty of appreciation and respect (Leo-food), and you'll find an endless font of silliness and affection that all seem typically Leonine. I've laughed harder in France than anywhere on earth.

My grandparents were Norwegian immigrants, so I'll hazard some guesses about the Norwegian national character. I think it has Taurus rising. Doane gives Norway's chart as June 7, 1905, 10:30 a.m., Oslo (Gemini Sun, Leo Moon, Virgo rising), although Norwegians themselves celebrate Norwegian Independence Day on May 17, when the Sun is in Taurus. Remember Garrison Keilor's "Norwegian bachelor farmers"? When Norwegians think of families and of where they're from, until quite recently they tended to think in terms of family *farms* (Taurus). Norwegian surnames are either patrynomic, after one's father, or place-names, usually after one's family farm or its locale. Most Norwegians are very fond of the out-of-doors, and are practically born wearing skis, a practical Taurean adaptation to a snowy climate. Trolls, almost the Norwegian national mascot in modern times, are distinctly earthy and Taurean, particularly in their earlier, larger, scarier forms. Norwegian mythology is very earth-centered (Taurus) and weather-influenced: the Earth is formed from the body of a frost giant. The Norse underworld is cold, not hot, in keeping with their climate. Traditional Norwegian food is Taurean: heavy on the butter and starches. And Norwegians have a reputation for being stoic and taciturn, while Taurus is the least verbal of the signs. Two of my favorite Norwegian jokes are "Did you hear about the Norwegian who loved his wife so much he almost told her?" and "How can you tell when you're talking to an extraverted Norwegian? He looks at *your* shoes." The question of Norway is particularly interesting, since Norwegian-American friends often marvel at how much the national character has changed since the Viking Age. Perhaps an entire people's Ascendant evolves over time, just as an individual's Ascendant does.

I have no exercises for you for this chapter, other than enjoying your own speculations about assigning an Ascendant to the national character of whatever cultures you know well.

CHAPTER TEN: THE ASCENDANT, SPECULATIONS ON PHYSICAL APPEARANCE, AND RECTIFICATION TIPS

This material about physical appearances has its own chapter because, since its topic is more externally oriented, it doesn't form a natural part of the Ascendant "cookbook" that appears in Chapter Twelve, and that is more oriented to the perspectives of evolutionary astrology.

Older astrology books often associate certain physical characteristics with each rising sign. However, many of those observations come from even older written material or traditions that drew from a mostly European and rather homogenous gene pool. For some modern data, as well as for an astonishing and illuminating visual astrology lesson, please go to www.astrofaces.com. Here's the blurb from their home page:

> Astrofaces is a research study seeking to verify Astrology for modern science with photographs of subjects grouped by the zodiac signs of their Sun, Moon & Ascendant. Do people who share the three most prominent factors in the chart resemble each other? Does the shape of time show in our faces?

Any visitor to astrofaces.com can submit photographs and birth data to the website, and the photos can be viewed by any combination of Sun, Moon or Ascendant. Perusing this fascinating website is well worth all the time you can spend there, including periodic return trips to check for new material. Its pictures are worth far more than the proverbial thousand words. The physical similarities that occur across racial lines are particularly striking. Steven and I are not connected with this website and don't know its owners; we simply found it while surfing one day.

I'm eager to see astrofaces.com collect so many photographs that a chapter such as this one, with its comments on the physical characteristics of different astrological configurations, might some day become superfluous. Please consider sending them your own photo and birth data; all the specifications they'll need are listed on their website.

In the meantime, I have no photo documentation for this book, but I do have some *subjective and anecdotal* observations I've gleaned from almost 24 years of doing face-to-face readings. *My comments by no means apply to all instances of a particular rising sign.* Remember that the Ascendant is a filter or a mask over the rest of the chart, and that the rest of the chart, particularly any planets that aspect the Ascendant, can almost always be sensed through that filter and can modify its expression.

From my experience doing rectifications, when an astrologer sometimes has to determine if a client has one of two adjacent signs rising, I've added a few tips for making such decisions. Obviously, far more than an assessment of a client's appearance comes into play during the complex work of rectification. However, I always ask for photographs of the client at different ages, so that I can make visual cues a small additional part of the rectification process.

Finally, even when astrologers don't have to do a rectification, they may sometimes need to make a judgment call between two possible Ascendants for a client. Those cases arise when a client has either 29 degrees of one sign or 0 degrees of the following sign rising. With such a chart, if the client's stated birth time is inaccurate by mere minutes, then a birth chart based on that inaccurate time may well show the wrong Ascendant.

If you're an astrologer dealing with such a situation, sometimes it will be abundantly clear which of the two possible Ascendants is correct as soon as you watch a client park, get out of the car and head for your office. Sometimes you'll get a good sense of your client's correct Ascendant during your initial chitchat with him or her. But other times, in order to determine what sign your client has rising, you'll have to ask some tie-breaking questions. What sort of questions? You might ask about your client's preferences and antipathies in relationships (the Descendant, always the sign directly opposite the Ascendant). You might inquire about others' first impressions of your client (the Ascendant). You might ask about his or her reported comfort level and behavior in various hypothetical situations that the Ascendant most typically handles: meeting new people; being interviewed for a job; navigating through a big office party; shopping in a crowded mall, etc.

Meanwhile, perhaps the following observations of mine will be helpful to you.

Aries rising: People with an Aries Ascendant often move quickly and can seem restless or impatient. They may talk rapidly, sometimes with a challenging or combative air underlying their statements. Their voices usually carry well. They can be easily irritated, or perceive conflicts where none were intended. They hate to wait. Their eyebrows can begin low over the inner corners of the eyes and arch sharply, even ending higher over the outer corners, almost like miniature ram's horns. The forehead may have modeling that follows this arch. Sometimes there are scars or bumps on the face or the head. The gaze is direct and the expression usually alert. Older astrology books mention a strong possibility of red hair, but again, the gene pool of the people upon which those observations were based was smaller then, and mostly European. There can be a red "aura" to this Ascendant, however, a strong, "don't mess with me" quality to its energy, far more so than with Pisces rising. When people with Aries rising enter a room, they seem to stake out territory in it, and they may drive very aggressively. Even allowing for differences in age and fitness levels, the body tends toward a leaner, more muscular structure. Unless clothing is being used to signal status or hierarchy, the Aries Ascendant often prefers non-restrictive, non-fussy garments.

Taurus rising: This Ascendant gives off an aura of the Immovable Object, in contrast to the impression of the Irresistible Force that Aries rising tends to give. The Taurus Ascendant's body is often solid or has round, endomorphic tendencies; the bones can be large and heavy. People with Taurus rising may blink less frequently than other rising signs do, and they're fond of gazing out of windows that offer a pleasant view, or gazing at floral arrangements or interesting colors or shapes in your office. Their expression is usually calm and ruminative or carries a certain mildness, and their eyes are often luminous. Frequently there are slow, deliberate movements and gestures, and a down-to-earth quality. These people like to set their own pace at whatever activity they're engaged in, and their pace can be slower than that of others performing the same task. Often they have a strong-looking throat and an appealing voice. They prefer their most comfortable and well-broken-in garments, or classic clothing in softer textures, nothing itchy or otherwise annoying. This Ascendant often seems at ease in its body, and as if all the senses are aware of all of the environment's sounds, smells, visuals and temperature. Given a choice of chairs or rooms, this person will go for comfort, natural lighting and fresh air. Children with this Ascendant may be very tactile, and very sensitive to odors and to the texture, color and taste of food.

Gemini rising: Where Taurus rising can seem rooted to the spot, Gemini rising can seem about to take flight. These people often fidget or appear nervous or easily bored. They can be very articulate or just very talkative and may interrupt frequently, or change subjects in mid-paragraph or even mid-sentence. They tend to be easily distracted, and their schedules may be packed. If any Ascendant can actually enjoy multi-tasking, it's Gemini. People with Gemini rising often notice virtually everything in their environment and may make comments about what they observe, particularly if anything has changed. They may crane their necks to read the titles of your books or CDs. They can be extremely curious and animated. They tend to relish verbal displays of wit and often try to engage others in as lively a conversation as possible. The expression is frequently humorous, the eyes bright, and the direction of the gaze often shifts. Sometimes the head is cocked to one side, and seldom held in the same position for very long. Often people with Gemini rising have long flexible hands and narrow fingers. Sometimes their dress is "youthful" for their age; frequently they appear younger than they are. Some Gemini Ascendants are so busy thinking that they're fairly oblivious to what they're wearing. They may be thin either from sheer nervous energy or because they forget to eat.

Cancer rising: Where Gemini rising can feel like a hyperactive adolescent who's dying to explore your office, someone with Cancer rising often seems cautious, guarded or even distant until he or she feels safe with you. Until then, these people watch you carefully, although they may try to conceal the fact that they're doing so. Seldom extraverts, they don't like having their personal space or their personal information invaded or even observed by strangers. However, they can quickly show sympathy toward anyone who's hurt or ill, and pets tend to feel safe around them. People with this Ascendant are often very sensitive to light, sound and temperature, easily startled and literally thin-skinned. They tend to be moody, although they may "clam up" and hide their feelings behind a poker face. One type is short and fleshy with soft thin hair, large eyes, a high forehead, a smallish mouth, and a round "Moon" face. This type retains fluid easily. A less common type is taller and rangier, with a craggy "Crab" face. Women with this Ascendant frequently have a prominent belly and larger than average breasts. Both men and women like to have water or another beverage close at hand. Their clothing is often loose and layered, as if hiding the body.

Leo rising: People with a Leo Ascendant are frequently tall, or their rather erect posture and poise are such that they seem taller than they actually are. Their self-presentation is memorable and can be dramatic; they tend to make an impression on others whether or not they've set out to do so. Especially in youth, they often have thick healthy hair and a strong upper body. The head can be long and carried up and forward, and the features well-defined. They seem to behold you and contemplate you, usually in an amiable way, rather than just look at you. They can dress rather flamboyantly, as if wearing a costume, and they often like bright colors. Where Cancer rising sometimes seems to be trying to disappear, literally or energetically, Leo rising gives the impression of abundant energy, warmth and confidence, often far more than they actually feel. If they're introverted, which is rare, they tend to be good at extraverted behavior when necessary. Once they're sure you're not laughing at them or disrespecting them—they hate having their dignity punctured—they love to laugh. They can be very gallant. They are most appreciative of genuine compliments and, unless they have a strong Saturn, they dislike being ignored, treated coldly or not noticed at all.

Virgo rising: The Virgo Ascendant's aura is initially down-to-earth, assessing and often a bit tentative, without Leo rising's larger-than-life presence. Their expression is frequently thoughtful or preoccupied, but as if they're actively analyzing something rather than just wool-gathering. Their gaze is often mobile and they may gesture a lot, but as if they're drawing conclusions rather than just taking in everything at once, as with Gemini rising. Even when fashions are slapdash, Virgo rising tends to be particular about its dress and grooming, and often has marked brand preferences. Men in particular may like small patterns on their clothing, especially geometric or abstract ones. Women frequently choose extremely coordinated outfits with complementary accessories and jewelry. If people with this rising sign are drowning in clutter, they're often unhappy about something. When unhappy, they may feel critical. Eyebrows tend to be well-defined, skin clear, pores small, nose long and mouth on the small side. They like to use their hands, often touching objects in the immediate environment. Less talkative than Gemini rising, they may give endless details when explaining something. Summarizing is a learned skill here, it doesn't come naturally. If holding in negative comments, they may purse or fold their lips as if literally pressing the words back.

Libra rising: Libra rising is far more tuned in to other people and more observant about them than is Virgo rising, who tends to be more judgmental and methodical. You can sense a Virgo Ascendant's wheels turning, but it's hard to tell what Libra rising is thinking behind its typical polish. They take time over their appearance, usually without Virgo's every-hair-microscopically-in-place look. Women tend to like "girly," very feminine and becoming outfits and makeup. This Ascendant is frequently extremely attractive or at least appealing, with symmetrical features, a quick smile, and a tendency to make eye contact and engage you personally. More often than not, they're photogenic. They tend to be easily influenced by their surroundings and companions, readily getting entrained into others' rhythms and even ideas. A visually appealing environment is highly important to them. As a friend with Libra rising said about his workshop—his *workshop!*—"It can be cluttered, but the space has to have a certain aesthetic." They often have strong social skills and may be exceptionally charming. All the Air Ascendants can be high-strung, but people with Libra rising tend to be so gracious and adaptable that it may take a while to tell if they're bored, displeased or don't agree with you, and even longer to realize how much they're actually evaluating what you're saying and how they'll respond.

Scorpio rising: While Libra rising's eye contact seems intended to disarm you and make friends with you, Scorpio rising stares into you and right through you. It's as if they don't want to miss anything, or they want to pin you to the spot and tattoo your skeleton with that penetrating gaze. The expression is frequently brooding, but even when this Ascendant is laughing, something about their energy says that they know some secrets and probably haven't revealed them all. If women with Scorpio rising wear makeup, they often go for a dramatic look with a lot of contrasts, and they tend to wear body-conscious, striking clothes. One type has dark eyes, olive skin, and visible pores sometimes even on the backs of the hands. If they're fair-skinned, the piercing gaze is still a giveaway. Leo rising makes an impact effortlessly, but with Scorpio rising the effect is more studied and deliberate. I suspect that people with Scorpio rising cannot imagine a world or a person without gender. They seem to want people to be aware of their sexuality as a basic part of who they are, regardless of whether they themselves are flirting or on the make, and this dynamic can leave other people confused about their intentions. They may be extraverted but are seldom very self-revealing, and they seldom trust easily. If they're tired, they can go out of their way to avoid people, probably because even when they've learned how to engage in lighter-hearted social behavior, it's hard for them to connect superficially, and connecting deeply takes extra energy.

Sagittarius rising: Where Scorpio rising tends to be self-aware and rather self-contained, Sagittarius rising's expression is generally open and earnest, and frequently good-natured. In younger people this quality tends toward exuberance, sometimes with a marked naïveté. Particularly when they're younger, before life has dealt them too many hard knocks, the look in this rising sign's eyes often says they enjoy a good joke. Laugh lines are frequently pronounced on older people, and all ages can have a contagiously hearty laugh. Even when the skin isn't fair, there's frequently a ruddy quality to it, what's sometimes called "high coloring." A love of good food may add weight if the years bring less activity. Otherwise, the body is often long-waisted and long-legged. Clothing is not fussy and is sometimes whimsical, as if these people are advertising their adventurous or humorous qualities—floppy hats, piratical scarves, clothes they can move in, etc. Hair is most often worn loose. Their body language tends to take up space—arms spread along the back of the sofa, feet stretched out in front of them. They often make sweeping, even "bull in a china shop" gestures, especially when pontificating about something. They frequently stride rather than just walk. Especially when younger, they can exhibit a breathtaking lack of social skills, but they're usually just ebullient, thoughtless or hard to repress, rather than maliciously rude or hostile.

Capricorn rising: The gaze is frequently very steady, although considerably less intense than that of Scorpio rising, and the expression is usually far more serious than that of Sagittarius rising. The nose tends to be on the long side, and the complexion is often darker than average. The whites of the eyes are usually not visible below the irises. These people frequently display an air of considering you carefully and evaluating your statements, although with Capricorn rising it seems to be your character itself that's being weighed, rather than Virgo rising's air of checking your facts. They are often highly organized and cautious. Like Cancer rising, this Ascendant can easily assume a poker face and betray little or anything of what this person feels. Capricorn rising takes up far less psychological and physical space than Sagittarius rising, who's often noisy and sometimes clumsy. The typical Capricorn Ascendant would make a great spy, or could be typecast as the butler in a classic English murder mystery, easily blending into the woodwork with appropriate, competent, unobtrusive behavior and few wasted motions. Clothing is often practical, well and simply cut, and muted or dark in color. There can be a preference for garments of good quality. These people tend to stick with styles that work for them rather than follow the trends. Accessories are seldom gaudy. Usually reserved, the Capricorn Ascendant seldom bubbles or chatters.

Aquarius rising. The eyes are often remarkably clear, and the gaze is far more detached than that of Capricorn rising, sometimes seeming almost icy or even shell-shocked. Usually the forehead is high and broad. The complexion tends to be good and the eyes wide-set. Aquarius rising people with Saturn stronger than Uranus in their natal charts tend to have more guarded, slightly suspicious and less "out there" energy than Aquarius rising people whose natal Uranus is stronger than their Saturn. The more Uranian types can seem wired, as if these people have stuck a finger into an invisible electric socket. Both Saturnine and Uranian types tend to like gadgets and often carry them (sophisticated PDAs, cell phones, pagers, etc.). Usually they are quick on the uptake and rather high-strung. As with Sagittarius rising, there can be a marked lack of social skills. With Sagittarius rising, that energy is rather clueless and seldom hostile, while Aquarius rising people tend to appear more as if they can't be bothered with trivialities and the rules don't apply to them. If the social skills are good, they're often accompanied by an offbeat sense of humor. Frequently these people are absent-minded, usually because they're thinking hard about something else rather than just zoning out. Clothing can either look as if they grabbed whatever was at the front of the closet, or as if they're deliberately using it to signal their individuality rather than following fashion dictates.

Pisces rising: The eyes are luminous, often large and dreamy, and seldom very deep-set. There's frequently a rather bemused expression and usually a kindly one. Sometimes all of this person's features seem slightly pulled toward the front of the face, and the mouth is usually well formed, if a bit on the small side. As with Aquarius rising, absent-mindedness is very common, but with Pisces rising it's as if this man or woman is involuntarily and hazily floating through another space-time continuum, rather than Aquarius rising's air of actively concentrating on something specific that just doesn't happen to be in the immediate surroundings. Usually the Pisces Ascendant's demeanor is warm, outgoing, open, a bit vulnerable and impressionable, and quick to empathize. Laughter is frequent and spontaneous; this Ascendant "gets the cosmic joke." Hands and feet are often small, and the skin can be a bit moist. There's frequently a lovely, gentle and extremely engaging smile, not so self-aware or deliberately charming as the Libran Ascendant's smile. People with Pisces rising think about their responses to questions longer than people with Aquarius rising do, and are far more apt to ask you where they should park or sit than Aquarian Ascendants are. There can be a taste for fabrics that drape well. Women tend to like pastels and shimmery shades and flowing garments.

I don't have exercises for further consideration of this chapter's material. Make frequent visits to www.astrofaces.com, or start your own photographic file of the faces of friends whose charts you know.

Now that we've examined the Ascendant from a very external, descriptive point of view, in the next chapter I'll discuss some far more philosophical speculation about this most physical part of the birth chart.

CHAPTER ELEVEN:
THE ASCENDANT AND EVOLUTIONARY ASTROLOGY

If I were a mathematician writing a formula on a blackboard for you, it would be helpful for you to know beforehand that I was working in base 10 rather than base 12, although there's nothing "wrong" with either base. If we were musicians about to improvise together, it would be convenient for you to know what key I was playing in before we started, although there's not any one "right" key. So let's begin this chapter with the principles or core perceptions of evolutionary astrology as formulated by Steven Forrest and Jeffrey Wolf Green.

Steven and Jeffrey have no monopoly on the term "evolutionary astrology," and some astrologers who use that term may not ascribe to their particular point of view. Astrology is a large and largely unregulated field. There's controversy about these principles. Even though you will read the word "fact" in the text below, Steven and Jeffrey are stating *principles*, not equations. Evolutionary astrology, as described by these principles, may not be provable in a left-brained, empirical, scientific-laboratory kind of setting. I'm *not* asking readers, students, clients or anyone else to believe or adhere to any of these principles. They are simply one of many ways of thinking about astrology. We all have every right to think for ourselves, and I have a strong bias that we all should—and that we shouldn't insist that others think exactly as we do, nor label them wrong if they don't. I state these principles here only so you'll understand my frame of reference for this particular chapter, and therefore be better able to adjust it to whatever your own frame of reference may be.

**The Principles of Evolutionary Astrology
as proposed by
Steven Forrest and Jeffrey Wolf Green, © 2000**

1. An acceptance of the fact that human beings incarnate in a succession of lifetimes.
2. An acceptance of the fact that the birth chart reflects the evolutionary condition of the soul at the moment of incarnation.
3. An acceptance of the fact that the birth chart reflects the evolutionary intentions of the soul for the present life.
4. An acceptance of the fact that the circumstances of the present life, both materially and psychologically, do not arise randomly, but rather reflect the evolutionary intentions and necessities of the soul.
5. An acceptance of the fact that human beings interact creatively and unpredictably with their birth charts, and that all astrological symbols are multidimensional and are modulated into material and psychic expression by the consciousness of the individual.
6. An acceptance of the fact that human beings are responsible for the realities they experience, both internally and externally.
7. A respectful intention to accept and support a person seeking astrological help, no matter the evolutionary state in which such an individual finds himself or herself.

Now I want to ask you a question. Why do we have Ascendants? Think about that question. Take it in and really *think* about it. Stop reading, close this book and speculate for a while.

Did you start wondering something along the lines of why we even have birth charts, let alone Ascendants? It's a short step from there to wondering "Why are we here at all? Why were we born?"

Perhaps you found yourself thinking about what the Ascendant is in literal terms. It's the degree and minute of the sign that was rising in the east *at the instant you were born*. If you didn't have an Ascendant, you wouldn't be here on this planet in a body. We have no way of knowing if you might be in some other form and some other place, but we do know that you wouldn't be in human form on planet Earth.

The Ascendant is, literally, the moment of your entry into this world, this body, this lifetime, this incarnation. The Ascendant is not your incarnation itself, but *the Ascendant is the vehicle through which you incarnate*. What does "vehicle" mean in this context? Container. Vessel. Engine. Carrier. The Ascendant isn't the journey itself, but it is the "spaceship" that carries us on the evolutionary journey of this lifetime.

I fear I'm belaboring simple points, and at the same time I fear I'm trying to address such great complexities that it's difficult to be concise or even coherent about them. Let's consider the same concepts from a slightly different approach.

Answer this question quickly: would you be here without your body, yes or no?

Unless you have ten planets in Pisces, you probably said "no." Then are you your body? If you aren't your body, then what are you other than your body, or apart from it, or beyond it?

I hope you're still with me, even if you're scratching your head. Like the Ascendant, the body is also a vehicle through which you incarnate, but *you* are not the same as your body. In parallel fashion, the Ascendant is not synonymous with the *person*, and it is not synonymous with the *body*, even though the Ascendant has much in common with the body.

As an evolutionary astrologer, I believe that everything in the birth chart can be used and is intended for one's continued evolution—one's long journey—through a succession of incarnations. The entirety of the birth chart describes this particular lifetime's leg of that long journey. The *vehicle* needed for this lifetime's leg of that journey must, in my opinion, be designed for the outer terrain which that journey will cross. *Therefore, the nature of the vehicle*—the Ascendant, its ruler, any first house planets, and any aspects to the Ascendant—gives us clues about *what that terrain will be.* According to evolutionary astrology, the nature of the Ascendant—the vehicle—also gives us clues about what that terrain *should* be.

To put these concepts still another way, the Ascendant governs our foreign relations—how we navigate through, interact with and behave in the outer world. The Ascendant's job description also includes the expression and/or protection of all the rest of our birth chart. In order for the totality of our birth chart to thrive, *we need to travel through the terrain described by the Ascendant.* Why? Because that particular terrain holds the outer experiences that will help the development and evolution of the totality of our birth chart. The Ascendant itself is also *our personal, custom-designed vehicle for navigating the very terrain that the Ascendant itself describes.* We can conceptualize the Ascendant as both the territory *and* the vehicle.

The Ascendant says a great deal about what sort of behavior will best serve us in this incarnation in this body. The Ascendant is not your ego (Sun), not your feelings (Moon), not your essence, not your spirit and not your Self. It is not the same thing as your body, although it has some definite parallels to your physical self—later in this chapter, we'll discuss the Ascendant and the body at more length. The Ascendant does, however, represent the *behavior* that will most help your ego, feelings, essence, spirit, Self and body all be healthy and flourish. *It also symbolizes what you need to do and where you need to go in order to practice that behavior.* With the Ascendant, it isn't so much "when in Rome, do as the Romans do," but rather "if you need to go explore Rome, then acting like a Roman will help take you there."

Here's a quick example. If you have Aries rising, you need to face (Ascendant) this world bravely (Aries). In order to develop this feisty (Aries) self-presentation (Ascendant), you would be wise to do things and go places that will require courage (Aries) from you. Therefore, you are driving a Land Rover (Aries Ascendant), not a sedate, middle-of-the-road Buick. Perhaps that Land Rover (Aries Ascendant) is meant to help protect a more inward, sensitive, even timid chart. Perhaps it's meant to help express a more dynamic, creative chart. Whatever the nature of the rest of your chart, a careful, comprehensive look at it through the lens of evolutionary astrology will reveal some excellent reasons why you were issued the Land Rover (Aries Ascendant) and not the Buick as your vehicle.

Like the Ascendant, the body is the vehicle through which we explore the world. But is the body, like the Ascendant, also *the territory in the world* that we should explore?

Not entirely. While I think that the significance of the astrological Ascendant has been downplayed and overlooked, I also think that we shouldn't *overemphasize* its importance. Why? Because down that road lie some of the same stumbling blocks inherent in the overemphasis of the persona and of the body. A person who overidentifies with the *Ascendant* runs the risk of becoming all style and no substance, of being no more than skin deep. There are psychological drawbacks and disadvantages to overidentification with the *persona,* as we discussed in Chapter Two. But what about someone who overemphasizes and overidentifies with the *body?*

Today's Western yoga teachers and bodyworkers might say that the body is *a* territory (as opposed to *the* territory) that we can explore, and that through the body we can understand much of our mind and spirit. "The body doesn't lie," they'll tell you. What do they mean by that? Basically, that the body's patterns of muscular tension and fascial tissue restriction or openness can signal something about the state of that person's psyche.

Certainly we can and do somatize our tensions and issues. To "somatize" something means to feel, express, store or carry that something in or through the body. For example, repressed or suppressed anger might be somatized as tight and painful shoulders, although that's not the only way or place that anger could be somatized. Earth Moons, along with hard aspects and major aspect patterns involving a planet or planets in Earth, seem particularly prone to somatization. But I'm not sure that everything we are and feel is written somewhere in the body, any more than I think that the body makes up the entirety of who we are.

Some of yesterday's more dualistic Christian sects might have said that not only is the body utterly separate from the spirit, it's also a trap and a snare for the spirit. "The body *is* a lie," they might have told you. What did they mean by that? Basically, that Spirit is good and Flesh is bad.

Some of that spirit/flesh split is still in operation today. That split appears to operate at the same time as, and to exist in some tension with, a certain identification of the spirit with the flesh. The rising tide of plastic surgery indicates an obsession with the *appearance* of the body: if the body doesn't look a certain rigidly defined way, then it's just not good enough.

An obsession with the body's appearance can be just as much a denial and a punishment of our natural physical selves—which include the ageing process and the occurrence of a wide variety of body types—as flagellation was a denial and a punishment of our bodies. An obsession with our appearance can also be connected to *our confusing our bodies with ourselves.*

Pema Chödrön, an American woman who is a Tibetan Buddhist nun, has written a wonderful book titled *No Time to Lose: A Timely Guide to the Way of the Boddhisattva* (Boston: Shambala, 2005). It's Chödrön's commentary and guide to an eighth century Buddhist text by the Indian sage Shantideva, but the points it makes are equally valid for non-Buddhists today. I cite a passage from this book below. The doubly indented lines that are preceded by the number 5.69, and the phrases in italics, are from the text by Shantideva. The text in parentheses is mine. Pema Chödrön writes:

> *The value of this human form* is in the way we use it. Without our bodies, we can't attain enlightenment. But if we live in hope and fear about its condition, it won't be a useful vehicle for getting to the other shore. . . Obsessing about how we look and feel wastes precious time and causes us to lose touch with the difficulties of others.

> 5.69
> So pay this body due remuneration,
> But then be sure to make it work for you.
> But do not lavish everything
> On what will not bring perfect benefit.

> If you're able to do so, you should *pay this body due remuneration*: nourishing foods, medicines and whatever else it needs—but draw a line about how much time you spend at the gym. It would also be wise to recognize "negative attachment." Denigrating the body is as futile and as much a distraction as pampering. . . It's a fine line . . . between taking pride in our appearance and being obsessed with it. Upliftedness (pride in our appearance) is a way of expressing our human dignity; obsession is a way of wasting our life. Gradually, we get clear about this difference.

"Getting clear about the difference" between honoring the *body* and obsessing over it has some parallels with learning to inhabit your *Ascendant* and using it to navigate through the world without overidentifying with it.

Compared to the volumes that have been written about the Sun and the Moon, there's relatively little astrological literature about the Ascendant, this vitally important feature of the birth chart. One reason for this relative lack of material might lie in some of the parallels between the body and the Ascendant. For a very long time, that perceived split between the body and the spirit was prevalent, or at least highly influential, in Western thought and in some Eastern thought as well. Perhaps that split has affected the importance that we assign to the Ascendant. Perhaps that's why we astrologers have paid relatively little interpretive attention to it. *Perhaps the body and the Ascendant are sufficiently interrelated that to neglect, suppress, distort or overemphasize the one incurs the risk of neglecting, suppressing, distorting or overemphasizing the other.* For whatever reasons, I suspect that the Ascendant carries profoundly more significance than many of us have assigned to it so far.

We've reached the end of this book's theoretical material. I have no real exercises for further study here, but I do want to ask you three "essay questions." They are interrelated, and over the course of our lives, we all have to answer them for ourselves.

1. How important is your Ascendant?
2. How important is your body?
3. How important is this incarnation?

The "cookbook" chapter that follows won't cover the Ascendant and purely physical appearances, since that more external, descriptive material was discussed in Chapter Ten. Instead, the "cookbook" chapter draws from the more internal and developmental perspectives of psychology (how the Ascendant can interact with the environment and with other people), and of evolutionary astrology—what this Ascendant-vehicle is here to learn, and what territory those lessons should cover.

CHAPTER TWELVE: THE ASCENDANT "COOKBOOK"

Before we begin the "cookbook," I'd like to point out that the signs that come earlier in the traditional Aries-through-Pisces order of the zodiac are often simpler *to explain* than the signs that come later, so the earlier signs' analyses may be briefer than those of the later signs. However, the fact that a rising sign may be simpler to explain does not mean that it's any less rich, challenging, complex or rewarding *to live* in a healthy and growth-oriented way.

The "cookbook" will include a discussion of what may happen with *overidentification* with each Ascendant. The opposing "Other" that I mention in each overidentification section corresponds to that Ascendant's Descendant. The Descendant is the sign directly opposite the Ascendant; as the Ascendant sign is rising, the Descendant sign is setting. In this "cookbook" discussion, the Other may be a romantic partner, a colleague at work, a close personal friend, an enemy or sometimes even a stranger. The Other may well not have the actual Sun sign of the Descendant that is opposite the Ascendant under discussion. He or she may merely be someone who responds with behavior reminiscent of that opposite sign, because an extreme manifestation of any Ascendant can temporarily polarize others into reacting with something of its Descendant's behavior.

If you're a beginner, or if you'd like a quick refresher on the pairs of opposite signs, here's a list:

Aries opposes Libra
Taurus opposes Scorpio
Gemini opposes Sagittarius
Cancer opposes Capricorn
Leo opposes Aquarius
Virgo opposes Pisces
Libra opposes Aries
Scorpio opposes Taurus

Sagittarius opposes Gemini
Capricorn opposes Cancer
Aquarius opposes Leo
Pisces opposes Virgo

Here's why I'm not covering what can happen with *underidentification* with the Ascendant: if someone underdoes their Ascendant, it doesn't really show up. It doesn't fully manifest. And it's hard to describe something that isn't there.

In general, people who seriously underdo their Ascendants have no "skin." They tend to *feel* vulnerable and to *act* uncentered, unsocialized, maladroit or goofy. As they try to bring their Ascendant into manifestation, they will probably demonstrate flashes of "overdoing" it, flashes which alternate with that generic, feral-child-sees-civilization-for-the-first-time, fish-out-of-water awkwardness of an underdeveloped Ascendant.

The end of the "cookbook" has a section about planets in the first house. The rising sign itself is the Ascendant, but planets in the first house are like alternate or additional masks that can and should be worn by that person as needed.

Finally, please keep in mind that although astrological "cookbooks" by their nature address just one configuration at a time, a human being's Ascendant never exists in a vacuum. In a reading, the Ascendant should be considered in the context of the living hologram *of the entire birth chart.* If you are giving an evolutionary interpretation of a birth chart, always ask yourself:

> * Why would someone with this birth chart need *this* particular rising sign to best further his or her evolution, and not one of the other eleven signs?
> * How does the vehicle of *this* particular Ascendant help this person with this birth chart fully incarnate in this lifetime?

* What sort of terrain does someone with this birth chart, who arrived equipped with *this* particular Ascendant-vehicle, need to travel?
* What sort of evolutionary food does someone with this birth chart and *this* Ascendant's "mouth" need? What sort of fuel does this Ascendant-vehicle need?

ASCENDANT IN ARIES:

The Symbols: This person has come into the world wearing the mask of the Warrior, the Daredevil, the Pioneer, and the Hero/Heroine. Other images for Aries include the Stuntman/Stuntwoman, the Adrenaline Junkie, the Athlete, and the Competitor. Lower level manifestations of this sign's energy might be the Rageaholic, the Stress Addict, the Bully, or the Reckless Fool.

The Style: This man or woman has reached an evolutionary stage where he or she must present a confident, assertive, energetic face to the world. The development of courage and the readiness to take risks are essential; so is the development of the will. Life must be confronted with pluckiness, if not boldness. These people should exit their lives able to *look* more fierce and to *act* more bravely than they did when they arrived here.

If the rest of the chart is more mild, then, like a dragon in a moat around a castle, the Aries Ascendant is intended to *protect* it. If the rest of the chart is dynamic, then the Aries Ascendant is intended to *express* it. For gentle souls and live wires alike, this rising sign's demeanor should convey the message: "Here is someone it would be unwise to cross."

If the childhood was difficult or dangerous, a stronger person may have decided to fight his or her way through life. Such a person may appear to have chips on both shoulders, until he or she learns that not all situations require such an edgy response. A more fragile person with such an upbringing may have decided that Life Equals Stress, and may behave nervously, defensively or with passive aggression until he or she learns to show more courage and confidence. Both types need some "turf" that feels like theirs, and need to defend it if it's genuinely threatened.

The Persona and the Other: the First House/Seventh House Axis:
People who *overidentify* with their Aries Ascendants may develop what some magazine editors I know jokingly call "Libra Deficit Disorder." The magazine editors were referring to writers who got nasty or even abusive when their submissions weren't immediately acknowledged, when any editing of their work was suggested, when their articles weren't mentioned on the cover, when their work was rejected for even the most valid and non-critical reasons, etc. All these reactions display a self-centered lack of awareness of other people (in this case, of the editors) as separate and sovereign human beings with their own needs and feelings, and with an agenda (in this case, for a certain issue or for the whole magazine) that may perfectly legitimately *not* match the agenda of the Aries rising person.

Someone who overidentifies with an Aries Ascendant can be blindingly self-centered and want to win, be first, be the best and be on top. Any disagreement or difference can be seen as an attack by the Aries rising person, and a vigorous counterattack can be made.

How might the Other react to such extreme behavior? It's possible that the Other may be polarized into various Libran responses.

The Other may say, "No relationship (Libra) is possible with a person who doesn't see enough beyond himself or herself to know that I'm a separate person with separate needs (Libra), and who isn't willing to negotiate (Libra). If I try to stay, I'll be bulldozed. I'm leaving."

The Other may instead react with Libran "sweetness," and placate, compromise, surrender, or otherwise perform some version of turning himself or herself into what the Aries rising person wants. Sometimes that placating behavior can be maintained for a long time. But when the Other can no longer maintain it, the Other may start to assert some selfhood. The Other may also start looking for kinder, gentler intimates who do acknowledge his or her existence as something other than a tool of the Aries rising warrior. And then the Aries rising person may become enraged at the Other's "betrayal."

These extreme behaviors are *not* the typical expression of a healthy Aries Ascendant. They are only what *may* happen with *overidentification* with this Ascendant. (Please see Chapter Two for a discussion of the dynamic of overidentification in this context.)

How might this dynamic be avoided?

If you have Aries rising, *listen* when your partner says, "Could we please talk about what *I* need? There are two of us in this relationship and we both have needs."

If you have Aries rising, *listen* when your partner says, "I think you might need to soften your stance here." Or when your partner says, "Why are you so angry? I think you might be overreacting." Try to see and acknowledge and respect your partner's point of view, even if you don't agree with it. You won't lose or surrender anything by doing so.

If you have Aries rising, think carefully about what most influences your choice of partner. Of course you're drawn to Libran graciousness, warmth and other-centeredness. In an evolutionary sense, you benefit from such qualities in your mate, so that your Warrior mask might learn some lessons in charm and negotiation from your partner's example. But are you looking *only* for a yes-man or a yes-woman, with no other criteria? History is full of tyrants who fell because no one dared to tell them what they needed to hear . . .

Of course you're drawn to Libran aesthetics and to beauty. In an evolutionary sense, aesthetics and beauty can help you learn what your Warrior energy might find worth preserving and protecting. Some cultures didn't teach a warrior the use of weapons until they'd taught the warrior to play an instrument or to dance—you didn't learn to destroy life until you'd learned to create. But is physical beauty *all* that matters to you? As a men's website says, "Beauty fades, but attitude is forever."

The Vehicle and the Terrain: Like it or not, this person has arrived on the planet with a vehicle—the Aries Ascendant—that is meant to move through life as a kind of ongoing Outward Bound experience. In other words, someone with Aries rising needs the terrain of risky, challenging or exciting situations, situations that create the possibility of a courageous response. The experiential fuel this Aries vehicle needs can be scary, and the terrain it should cover is anywhere that quickens the "driver's" pulse. Remember, however, that what scares a double Cancer, say, can be very different than what scares a double Sagittarius, and adjust your thoughts about that Aries-rising charged terrain according to the rest of the chart.

Fragile flower or King Kong, the Aries Ascendant's journey through life is like a hero's journey through terrain that feels dangerous to that particular individual. *The Lord of the Rings* is a hero's journey that has found its way into popular culture, and it can give us plenty of analogies for this process. The Ring must be taken to the Aries Ascendant's particular Mount Doom, and plenty of Black Riders and Gollums must be faced along the way. If Aries rising can learn to equip its vehicle with a few Elfin swords that glow blue when Orcs are about, so much the better.

Yet the Aries Ascendant's greatest enemies are his or her own fears and potential for cowardice. What if Aries rising chickens out and won't equip itself (vehicle) with enough assertiveness to go to Mordor (terrain)? Then Mordor will come to him or her. It might be in the person of The Boss from Hell (Capricorn or Virgo Sun or Moon, perhaps, or emphasized sixth or tenth houses). It might be in the person of The Spouse From Hell (Libra or Scorpio Sun or Moon, perhaps, or emphasized seventh or eighth houses). It might be in the person of The Child From Hell (Cancer Sun or Moon, perhaps, or emphasized fourth or fifth houses). A wise use of the Aries Ascendant's energy is *choosing one's own quests bravely*—quests which are typically described by the rest of the chart and which will require the use of Aries-rising courage to complete—rather than letting life assign those quests in the form of ordeals.

Staying Comfortable in the Body: Keep the body strong and confident in age-appropriate and realistic ways. With that caution in mind, this person may have a taste for competitive sports or martial arts, and benefit from them. Remember, however, that people with this Ascendant can sometimes regard physical weakness itself as an enemy, and try to push themselves (or others!) mercilessly. We all have different physical abilities and constitutions, and Aries rising does well to recall that this Ascendant does not make one the Bionic Man or Woman.

Images for a Costume: Any military uniform. Any sports uniform or gear. Hunting garb. Davy Crockett buckskins. A stunt person's protective gear. Something red. A suit of armor. A helmet. A police or SWAT team uniform. Brass knuckles and an Uzi. Anything that makes a person look larger and scarier.

Images for the Vehicle: A Ferrari. A muscle car. An armored Hummer. A tank. A Harley. A bomber. A highly trained war horse. A very maneuverable fighter spacecraft bristling with photon torpedoes. Hans Solo's *Millennium Falcon* from the first Star Wars movie. The fighter jet that Luke Skywalker flies into the Death Star. A Klingon Bird of Prey.

Images for the Terrain: A racetrack. A war zone. A mountain-climbing expedition. A martial arts studio. An Olympic arena. A dive to check out reports of sea monsters. An asteroid, hurtling toward the earth, carrying nuclear warheads that need disarming. The set of a dangerous film stunt. Any place that frightens a person with this Ascendant.

The Ambassador's Host Country—Mars's House Position:
Since this is where Aries rising gets the most assertiveness training lessons, it's a very important part of the terrain. Here is where the Aries Ascendant should most avoid chickening out in any fundamental way. We covered some of this material in the example in Chapter Six.

Mars in the first house: A particularly vibrant expression of Aries rising is needed here, as if the person needs to "stay in uniform." A double dose of experiences such as literal assertiveness training classes, Outward Bound expeditions, adventure travel or martial arts classes might be indicated. If this person *overdoes* the Ascendant, we might see a need for anger management classes or stress reduction techniques.

Mars in the second house: In order to have healthy self-esteem, this person needs Mars experiences (adventures, assertiveness and, probably, physical exercise: Mars needs to move). Also, this individual must take pro-active control of his or her financial life (second house). The wimpier this person feels, the lower the self-esteem will be, and the narrower the opportunity space he or she may allow himself or herself.

Mars in the third house: Verbal assertion and self-defense need to be sharp here. This house position of Mars as Ascendant ruler benefits from developing an active, dynamic, punchy style of communication, and from claiming the right to a life filled with *interesting* experiences, not just a horrendously busy life. If this person fails in these tasks, he or she could suffer too much stress from sheer cognitive overload.

Mars in the fourth house: This Aries rising person needs to avoid letting a parent dominate him or her, either in person or by influence. (This dynamic includes behavior that's a total reaction against that influence, which is being just as affected by it as is completely yielding to it.) He or she should set healthy boundaries in family life. He or she must be able to defend the home environment, and claim a home and home life that work well and peacefully, lest they become a chronic battlefield.

Mars in the fifth house: A creative outlet is good for this individual, particularly one that involves performance. This person needs to defend the right to have some recreational, unstructured, non-goal-oriented time, no matter how busy and productive our culture presses us to be. He or she should set boundaries very early in a new relationship or a new friendship, or run the risk of being bullied.

Mars in the sixth house: Finding and developing the right craft will require a certain amount of sheer courage. This person must be careful not to let overwork wear him or her down—the ability to say "no," and to claim what's wanted and needed at work, is essential to job satisfaction and perhaps even physical health. The right mentors should model this behavior in a constructive way. Otherwise, this person could be the punching bag of the office bullies.

Mars in the seventh house: This individual benefits immensely from relationships with spunky, direct, energetic people—and if he or she doesn't develop enough assertiveness to keep from being bulldozed by them, there could be ongoing trouble and stress in relationships. To that end, it's important to settle differences quickly, rather than letting them fester.

Mars in the eighth house: This person's natural mate, and the friends who make the deepest psychological impact on him or her, are towers of strength. That profound level of eighth-house intimacy can spook this person. And it should, if he or she doesn't develop enough strength to hang in there with such scary folk and, when they need to hear it, to "tell the truth and shame the devil."

Mars in the ninth house: The philosophy of life that works best for this person could be summarized as "Feel the fear, and do it anyway." A life whose major decisions are based on fear is no life at all here.

This person may need to insist on the right to follow wherever his or her vibrant and even danger-courting star leads, or risk being bored half to death, finding life meaningless, and being bitter about it.

Mars in the tenth house: As a "cosmic job description," this person should symbolize courage and energy, or adventurousness, leadership or even heroism to the community. If he or she's not brave enough to claim that role, a less healthy manifestation is possible: that of the victim. If he or she is less cowardly but still claims the wrong role, we might see the town bully or abrasive malcontent.

Mars in the eleventh house: To accomplish goals that are truly meaningful to this individual, he or she needs "troops": feisty live wires who aren't afraid to make noise and take up space. A healthy response here means that this person will get pluckier with age, while a less than optimal response may leave him or her a stressed and contentious senior citizen.

Mars in the twelfth house: This person's inner guru is a mystical warrior. The right use of courage, willpower and action can be a profound aid in the development of his or her spiritual life. On the other hand, these people could be spurred toward spiritual growth by the aftermath of losing their tempers in highly embarrassing ways. The choice is theirs . . .

ASCENDANT IN TAURUS:

The Symbols: This person has come into the world wearing the mask of the Earth Mother/Earth Father, the Indigenous Tribesperson, the Pagan, the Sensualist, the Farmer, or Salt of the Earth. Other images might include the Ecologist, the "Totem Animal," the Granola Person or the Field Hippie. Lower level manifestations of this sign's energy might include the Stubborn Mule, the Arch-Conservative, the Lazy-Bones and the Materialist.

The Style: This man or woman has reached an evolutionary stage where he or she must present an earthy, solid, common-sensical and centered face to the world. The more fully these people inhabit their physical selves and make friends with all their senses, the better. Life should be met as a *primate*—a human, intelligent, civilized and soulful primate, but a primate nonetheless, someone who has not lost touch with his or her instinctive side. If the rest of the chart is more mental, emotional or fiery, the Taurus Ascendant is intended to protect it and ground it. If the rest of the chart is kinesthetic and pragmatic, the Taurus Ascendant is intended to help express it. In either case, this rising sign's demeanor should convey the message: "Here is a person capable of being practical, with both feet planted firmly on the ground."

If the childhood was difficult or dangerous, a stronger person may have used Taurean stubbornness to survive and therefore may need to learn that not all compromises are dangerous. A more fragile Taurus Ascendant with such an upbringing may become very focused on safety and security. Both types need calm and stability in their lives, and do well to avoid letting material comfort and pleasure become all-important ends in themselves.

The Persona and the Other—the First House/Seventh House Axis:

How does someone who *overidentifies* with a Taurus Ascendant appear? Imagine that the instinctive side is more in control than the human side. What are such people like? Earthy. Dominated, or at least strongly influenced, by primate appetites, instincts, impulses and drives. Unwilling to think through the consequences of their actions or inaction. "I *will* have a baby, even though I'm nineteen years old and penniless, and its father doesn't want either the child or me as a partner." Do you think this young woman will give a child a good start in life? "I would rather sleep late than exert myself to go to work today, although I have to earn money and have no other prospects at the moment." Think this person will keep that job long? "I want that food, or that money, or that sexual partner—although I'm obese, or it isn't really my money, or it's inappropriate or even dangerous to sleep with him or her." Care to speculate about the long term health of this person's body, honesty, finances and relationships? Someone whose Taurus Ascendant is overfunctioning may not be giving enough thought to the long term consequences of his or her actions. Humans can think long term (although they don't always do so). Animals can't and don't.

Another possible manifestation of an overfunctioning Taurus Ascendant is a desire for material comfort and security at the cost of all other values—a comfortable nest comes before ethical practices at work. Another manifestation is an ingrained and stubborn distrust of any change whatsoever, to the point where anything new, however beneficial, is suspect. Animals are creatures of habit . . .

These examples are of course *not* the typical expressions of healthy Taurus Ascendants. They are only what may happen with *overidentification* with this Ascendant. (Please see Chapter Two for a discussion of the dynamic of overidentification.)

If these extreme expression of Taurus rising occurs, how might the seventh-house Other react? It's possible that the Other may be polarized into various Scorpio responses.

The Other may say, "How do you think I feel when you can't see further than the end of your nose? What were you *thinking* when you called in 'sick' right before that deadline when your office needed everyone, and you got fired? You could have caught up on your rest this weekend." The Other may say, "What were you *thinking* when you slept with her and lost my trust? I don't care if she showed up naked on our doorstep. Can't you think of anything beyond your whimsy of the moment?"

Imagine that your therapist was really angry at you, and not bound by professional ethics to contain that feeling. The Other may perform a Scorpio-style and not particularly tactful (or even accurate) "psychoanalysis" of the Taurus Ascendant: "It's because your parents overindulged you." The Other may browbeat the Taurus Ascendant: "Will you wake up and grow up? I have a libido too, but I don't give it free rein all the time." Or: "You are so naïve! Can't you see that life is complicated and involves change? We all have to do things we don't feel like doing sometimes."

Taurus rising may feel defensive, particularly since this sign's more instinctual world view doesn't readily encompass complexities. In that case, Taurus rising may dig in his or her heels. "I'm not the mental case you make me out to be. One of us must be wrong and one of us must be right, and you're wrong to attack me in such a nasty way. So I must be right. So there."

How might this dynamic be avoided?

If you have Taurus rising, *listen* when your partner says, "I think this situation might be more complex than you think." No matter how much you hate "processing things," ask what factors your partner thinks you're overlooking. You're quite capable of being practical in the here-and-now; all you have to do is think a little bit ahead, too. Entertain the possibility that some changes are actually good for you.

If you have Taurus rising, think carefully about what most influences your choice of partner. Of course you're drawn to Scorpionic intensity and emotional depth. In an evolutionary sense, you can benefit from such qualities in your mate so that your Earth Mother/Father mask will become more aware of life's more complex and problematic realities—passion, psychological growth, the existence of predators who don't have your best interests at heart, etc. But are you looking *only* for someone to handle all the areas that make you physically or emotionally uncomfortable? You can stretch enough to learn to handle those areas too.

The Vehicle and the Terrain: A person with Taurus rising arrived on the planet with a vehicle—the Taurus Ascendant—that's meant to move through life as an ongoing act of physical, sensory, kinesthetic *grounding*. What does that mean? Not losing touch with one's instinctive side. Cultivating a visceral, body-centered calm and a centeredness in one's own skin. Eating nourishing food when we're hungry, not when the clock says it's time to eat. The experiential fuel this Taurus vehicle needs includes anything that connects us to the rhythms of Nature, both within us and around us. The terrain it should cover is anywhere that animal-sense of self can not only come into play, but also flourish.

These people should not spend all their lives indoors. Claiming quiet, non-verbal time and having pets are exceptionally good for them. Downtown Manhattan during rush hour is not. The Taurus rising path should not seek to transcend the body nor to mortify the flesh—this path goes into and through the body; it *uses* the body. As long as one doesn't get too lost in one's primate nature, the path almost *is* the body. Treat the body as one would as a beloved animal friend, with the right diet, exercise, sleep, air, light and environment for that particular animal. The Taurus-rising spaceship runs on organic technology.

This rising sign's occupational hazards include the potential for the human's becoming submerged in the animal. Ideally, the human nature and the instinctive side, the animal nature, are forging a bond and becoming partners, rather than only the human or only the animal staying in charge. Another hazard is a desire for comfort or stability at all costs. A wise use of the Taurus Ascendant's energy is to choose how best to be fully present in the body and the senses, without losing the ability to function as an intelligent and reflective human being.

Staying Comfortable in the Body: Taurus rising wrote the book on this one, and little guidance is needed here. Ask your "inner animal" how it feels about this activity, that bedtime, this diet, that person. If you ask seriously, and take time to listen for the answer, your inner animal will always tell you. When in doubt, go for a walk. Do some stretching. Lie down and figure out where you're physically tense, and why. Your inner animal may not use words—it may use a burst of energy, or a yawn, or a headache. But it will tell you what you need to know.

Images for a Costume: Any indigenous people's costume. A loincloth. A farmer's overalls. A sculptor's smock. Comfy, broken-in clothing made from natural materials. "Earth mother or father" garb. Yoga gear. A garland of flowers. A Green Man costume. A park ranger's uniform. Clothes suitable for dancing around a Maypole.

Images for the Vehicle: A bicycle. A paddle boat. An easy-gaited horse, with or without a buggy. Something in which your body participates, and which doesn't move too fast for you to notice the scenery. As the proverb says, "The soul travels at the speed of a camel." A Prius. A car that runs on recycled oil or other alternative, organic fuels. A Subaru Forester.

Images for the Terrain: A yoga class. A Feldenkrais, Alexander or body-mind centering class. A long leisurely hike. An easy-to-reach campground. A road gently winding through sunny farmland. A screened-in, candle-lit porch in the summer rain. Anywhere that "chicken soup wisdom" would come in handy. A place one has to navigate by using one's senses, body and instincts.

The Ambassador's Host Country—Venus's House Position:
    Here is where someone with Taurus rising needs to be very mindful of maintaining a well-working partnership between the human and the inner animal . . .
Venus in the first house: This person needs an extra-calm expression of Taurus rising, with plenty of experiences that explore and affirm the senses. He or she does well to cultivate an art form that resonates with Taurus: music, dance, sculpture. Stable and stabilizing relationships with grounded individuals are also a plus. If this person

overdoes the Ascendant, he or she could get lost in the senses, or be so focused on comfort and pleasure that laziness or materialism become risks.

Venus in the second house: With Venus here, in order to have healthy self-esteem, a person with Taurus rising needs to develop good relating skills, and a creative outlet would be a real help as well. So would feeling poised and attractive at many levels, not just physically. So would enjoying the aesthetic side of life. However, care should be taken not to equate one's self-worth with one's appearance, possessions or partners.

Venus in the third house: Someone with Taurus rising and Venus in the third house can enjoy cultivating the communicative arts. He or she does well to communicate graciously and charmingly, in order to build calm, harmonious relationships. "A soft answer turneth away wrath"—but a soft answer isn't always called for, so this person should also learn when it's appropriate to negotiate or set boundaries in order to preserve the peace.

Venus in the fourth house: A Taurus Ascendant with Venus here benefits from a beautiful and soothing home, and prefers a peaceful home life. However, understanding one's family of origin is more important than maintaining peace at all costs there. Particularly if it's hard to leave the nest, this person does well to have a circle of friends and/or a present-day family who are loving, supportive and grounding, and who don't indulge in needless dramas.

Venus in the fifth house: With Venus here, a Taurus Ascendant needs to claim a certain amount of spontaneity, pleasure and "down time" in his or her life, and to avoid a schedule jammed with nothing but grinding responsibilities. Exploring creativity and sharing it in some form are both important. So is "falling in like" with aesthetically-minded and relaxed souls, and enjoying their company.

Venus in the sixth house: Someone with Taurus rising and this Venus placement does well to have meaningful work that allows him or her to use creativity, an eye for beauty, relating or counseling skills, or all of the above while on the job. A harmonious working environment is important. Mentors or protegés should be gentle, gracious, well-intentioned people.

Venus in the seventh house: With Venus here, this person benefits from relationships (marriage, partnerships, friendships) with warm, poised, charming and aesthetically sensitive people. Ideally, such partners should be other-centered and affiliative rather than self-centered, vain or spoiled. If the Taurus-rising person feels truly *seen* by his or her intimates, and able to relax in their presence, those are good signs.

Venus in the eighth house: A Taurus Ascendant with Venus in this house of psychological intensity needs to feel that the bond with the mate involves romance, tenderness, and great mutual sensitivity and consideration, as well as the physical connection. People of all style but no substance—slick charmers, lounge lizards, gold diggers—should be avoided, as should people who are attached to melodrama. Creativity and empathy are pluses.

Venus in the ninth house: With Venus here, this person's philosophy of life could be *ars longa, vita brevis* (art is long, life is short). Not just art and aesthetics but also relationships—simple, warm, uncomplicated Taurean connectedness—provide the greatest meaning to this individual's life. Once in a while these people and their partners should visit a museum, a national park or some other place they find lovely, just for the soul-soothing beauty of it.

Venus in the tenth house: People with Taurus rising and this placement of Venus do well to have a career, public identity, vocation or avocation that lets them use their Venus energy: counseling, sales, public relations, etc., or any of the arts. They are representing Venus to their community. They need to avoid highly stressful or combative work, and do better with jobs where they can experience a calm sense of "flow."

Venus in the eleventh house: With Venus here, a Taurus Ascendant needs associates who promote the healthy and ongoing development of his or her Venus function: artists, counselors, diplomats, etc. His or her goals should allow for the increasing importance of relatedness, community, aesthetics and creativity as he or she ages. **Venus in the twelfth house:** Someone with Taurus rising and this placement of Venus needs some quiet, meditative, contemplative time, perhaps alone, perhaps with a friend or a partner, perhaps while pursuing an art form. All relationships and all creativity are grist for the mill of spiritual development and mystical awareness here, so care should be taken not to approach those areas of life from a purely egocentric point of view.

ASCENDANT IN GEMINI:

The Symbols: This person has come into the world wearing the mask of the Perceiver, the Communicator, the Observer and the Storyteller. Other images for Gemini include the Questioner, the Journalist, the Student and the Information Junkie. Lower level manifestations of this sign's energy include the Trickster, the Eternal Adolescent, the Chatterbox and the Pedant.

The Style: This man or woman has reached an evolutionary stage where he or she should present an alert, articulate and perceptive face to the world. The development of objectivity and the ability to process lots of information are essential. Life should be faced with curiosity and open-mindedness. If the rest of the chart is highly sensitive and subjective, the Gemini Ascendant is intended to give it some objectivity and some protective coloration. If the rest of the chart is more earthy and/or fixed, the Gemini Ascendant is intended to help it loosen up. If the rest of the chart sparkles and scintillates, this Ascendant is intended to help express it. In any case, this rising sign's demeanor should convey the message: "Here is an inquisitive, articulate person who notices everything, who can think on his or her feet."

If the childhood environment was chaotic, it can be particularly difficult for a Gemini Ascendant to trust his or her perceptions and to sort out where the truth and the solid ground lie. Such a person may even be uncomfortable in a *non*-chaotic environment, until he or she does some psychological excavation work and realizes why, and that a more stable setting can be good for him or her. If the family refused to communicate, a stronger person may grow up starved for an audience, any audience, willing or not. A more fragile person may so fear or expect to be ignored that he or she may hesitate to speak. All of these types do well to learn that real communication is honest and is a two-way street, or it isn't truly communication.

The Persona and the Other—the First House/Seventh House Axis:

People who *overidentify* with their Gemini Ascendants may strike others as hyperactive, scattered, motor-mouthed or all of the above. They never stop moving. They never stop talking. They may have a fine thinking function, but seldom do they see anything through to completion. All too distractable and easily bored, off they go in pursuit of the next interesting idea, experience or person that happens to catch their eye.

People who are overdoing this Ascendant can often switch sides in a debate with such facility that it's impossible to tell what they really believe. They may not know for certain what they believe either, although they can enjoy the sheer intellectual feat of juggling facts and figures. *Belief* isn't the same thing as *thought*. Someone overdoing this Ascendant may seem to be trying to turn himself or herself into a thought form. The world is made only of thoughts, perceptions and observations—"I think, therefore I am." Dextrous and facile at sorting through and presenting various perceptions, they can rationalize, or appear to believe whatever's expedient at the moment. Feelings and values and practicalities can all be left aside.

These examples are of course *not* the typical expressions of healthy Gemini Ascendants. They are only what may happen with *overidentification* with this Ascendant. (Please see Chapter Two for a discussion of the dynamic of overidentification.)

If these extreme expressions of Gemini rising occur, how might the seventh-house Other react? It's possible that the Other may be polarized into various extreme Sagittarian responses.

The Other may pontificate, moralize or preach (Sagittarius): "I can see you're only looking for the main chance. If you don't know what's right and wrong, I do, so just listen to me for a minute."

The Other may join the Gemini Ascendant's marathon of experience-gathering. Both Gemini and Sagittarius can live at a pace that exhausts the rest of us. For a while. Sooner or later, though, the Other will say, "*Why* (Sagittarius) are we doing this to ourselves? We never stop long enough to process anything. Is this just busyness for the sake of busyness?"

The Other may get frustrated at Gemini's sheer verbal barrage. "Shut up! Why do you put up this smokescreen of words all the time? What's your point (Sagittarius)? Do you even believe (Sagittarius) any of what you're saying?"

Gemini rising, hurt or perplexed, may retreat into more rationalizations. How might this dynamic be avoided?

If you have Gemini rising, *listen* when your partner says, "Could we slow down, please? I can't socialize seven nights out of seven. I need some down time." Or when your partner says, "I'm hearing lots about what you're *thinking,* but I still have no idea what you feel." Or when your partner says, "I really need a promise from you here, and this is why." Try to see and acknowledge your partner's point of view, even if you don't agree. Resist the reflex to poke holes in your partner's arguments just because you can. Sometimes the needs of the relationship matter more than playing devil's advocate. Sometimes mates need to take leaps of faith—in each other.

If you have Gemini rising, think carefully about what most influences your choice of partner. Of course you're drawn to Sagittarius's need to derive meaning from life. In an evolutionary sense, you need to learn from Sagittarius's quest for meaning and from Sagittarius's exploration of the various cultural and philosophical *patterns* that explain reality to him or her. That quest counters and balances your own need for sheer *data*. But are you looking *only* for someone to write editorials for you? Or have you decided you'll stick with the learning/listening/reading side of the two-way street of communication, while you let the Other do all the teaching, talking and writing, because it's too much work to organize your thoughts into communicable patterns? Of course you're drawn to Sagittarius's need for experience and for robust engagement with life. But are you looking *only* for someone to potentiate your own desire for a steady diet of new experiences?

The Vehicle and the Terrain: Someone with this rising sign has arrived on the planet with a vehicle—the Gemini Ascendant—that is meant to move through life as a vast experiment in perception, open-mindedness and communication about The Mystery. What is The Mystery? The entire cosmos and everything in it. In other words, people with Gemini rising need terrain that fascinates them, that gets all their perceptive faculties wide open, that creates the possibility of an alert, objective response. The goal is to keep asking ever more interesting questions during this life-long fact-finding mission, not to come up with immutable answers. The experiential fuel this Gemini vehicle needs can be stimulating, puzzling, even bewildering, and the terrain it should cover is anywhere that gets the driver wondering about something.

These people need an environment that is the antithesis of boring, an environment where no one tells them how to think or what to believe, where there are no forbidden questions. Questioning *everything* is a good Gemini rising strategy. So is facing life with one's mind as *tabula rasa,* the proverbial blank slate, even though it can be hard to keep those slates uncluttered with the passage of time. What will help? Joseph Campbell advised us to follow our bliss, but Gemini rising needs to follow its curiosity.

Occupational hazards of a Gemini Ascendant include mistaking oneself for no more than a data-processing machine. This rising sign must remember to slow its pace sufficiently to eat nourishing food, to get sufficient rest and, as we'll see in a moment, to get enough exercise. Another risk this Ascendant can run is, to put it simply, thinking too much and not allowing feelings enough latitude. Some decisions may be emotionally necessary—such as getting a new kitten when your child is grieving a deceased pet—even when they aren't the most logical option. Another hazard is juggling the facts in such a way that Gemini rising plays fast and loose with the truth. Another risk (shared with Sagittarius rising) can be such fear of boredom or restriction that this Ascendant avoids any commitments, even such life-enhancing ones as undertaking a course of study that will lead to a career well-suited for this person, or committing to an intimate partner who's sane, stable and clearly a soul mate.

Staying Comfortable in the Body: Gemini rising is very mentally oriented, and does well to remember that the brain is a physical organ that is affected by the body's health. Also, a healthy body can gather lots of interesting experiences; an unhealthy one finds its options more limited. This Ascendant needs exercise to keep the body and the mind healthy; it needs to move. Otherwise, people with a Gemini Ascendant can get cut off from their own bodies, and nervous tension can build up in their physical selves long before they become aware of it. Think of them as having the racehorse or greyhound version of the nervous system: Gemini rising needs to "run," too.

Images for a Costume: A messenger bag and winged shoes. A student's backpack, cell phone, PDA, wi-fi-equipped laptop, sneakers and ink-stained fingers. A journalist's interview-recording gear. A "youthful" outfit. Clothing that lets these people move as fast as they want to, with a little notebook to jot down their thoughts, or a voice-activated tape recorder so they don't have to slow down to write.

Images for the Vehicle: A hovercraft. A racecar with high horsepower, a low turning radius and road-hugging tires. A spaceship with lots of communication gear and data collection and study devices. Anything that moves fast and with multidirectional capability. Since the third house of "short journeys" has a natural association with Gemini, anything that can speed up a short trip: a bicycle, a Segway, a skateboard.

Images for the Terrain: A research library or laboratory. An Internet host's computer room. A switchboard. A place that promotes cognitive overload. A racquetball court. A litter of kittens in a bathtub full of ping-pong balls. A place where one must stay maximally alert and aware of all stimuli and details: an air traffic control tower, rush hour traffic in Calcutta.

The Ambassador's Host Country—Mercury's House Position:
Mercury's house position is where a Gemini Ascendant most needs to stay extremely open-minded, enjoy a multiplicity of interesting situations, and avoid boredom if at all possible.
Mercury in the first house: This person needs a particularly vivid expression of Gemini rising, with all the perceptive faculties working at maximum. A double dose of fascinating, intriguing experiences and ideas helps this person spend as much time as possible being *amazed* by life. Developing excellent communication skills is a good means to that end. Someone who overdoes a Gemini Ascendant with

a first house Mercury risks getting cognitive overload, or becoming stuck on either information-input mode or information-output mode. **Mercury in the second house**: With Mercury here, this person's perceptive and communicative faculties can help him or her with self-esteem. This really has very little to do with having a high IQ or earning postgraduate degrees. Instead, it has to do with using whatever intellect one has to *notice* the world and to *wonder* about it. Care should be taken not to rack up Mensa memberships or go after others with an intellectual killer instinct merely to prop up one's self-worth.

Mercury in the third house: Someone with Gemini rising and Mercury in the third needs to focus on the communicative side of this Ascendant. Reading, writing, lecturing, listening, the Internet, photography—any of the ways we communicate could be important here. Care should also be taken to cultivate an objective, unprejudiced, curious attitude toward all the information, experiences and people the Gemini Ascendant encounters.

Mercury in the fourth house: This person benefits from a stimulating, information-intensive home environment with plenty of books, Internet access, interesting conversations at dinner, etc. It's also wise to spend some time figuring out how one's family of origin affected one's communicative style, open-mindedness, and attitudes toward learning. We don't always have to think exactly as our families did.

Mercury in the fifth house: A Gemini Ascendant with a fifth house Mercury needs to have some experiences and explore some ideas *purely for the pleasure of it.* Using one's mind is *fun* for these people, and without some fun in life, we all wither. These people should attend lectures on any topic that interests them, take up chess or backgammon or video games, etc. Clues that a new relationship could last and be meaningful are that the partner also likes to use his or her mind, and that their conversations are an ongoing source of delight.

Mercury in the sixth house: This person does well to have meaningful work that allows him or her to use perceptiveness, open-mindedness, an eye for detail, and communication skills. Too much on-the-job routine can be deadening here. If Mercury isn't used in the office, these people still need a Mercurial skill: speaking, writing, or possibly something requiring good hand-eye coordination. Mentors and protegés should be chosen with attention to their objectivity, curiosity and desire to keep learning.

Mercury in the seventh house: With Mercury here, this person benefits from relationships (marriage, partnerships, friendships) with quick-witted, articulate people with whom there is excellent communication. Someone once said, "Never marry anyone who is not a friend to your joy," but in this case we can say, "Don't marry anyone who's not a friend to your curiosity." Ideally, the partner is flexible and responsive, but not immature or overly glib.

Mercury in the eighth house: A Gemini Ascendant with this Mercury placement needs to feel that the bond with the mate involves both great mental rapport, and the ability to discuss and process eighth house issues (sexuality, death and dying, the deep unconscious, one's wounds and "shadow" issues) without too much rationalizing, defensiveness or dancing away from hard topics. Time spent exploring and observing these areas on one's own is a huge stabilizer for this person, too.

Mercury in the ninth house: The philosophy of life that works best for this person could be summarized as "Give me something to wonder about." Their guiding star (ninth house) is Mercury, and the development of their full observational and communicative capacities will help life feel maximally worth living to them. Too much avoidable boredom is their soul-poison.

Mercury in the tenth house: People with Gemini rising and this placement of Mercury do well to have a career, public identity, vocation or avocation that lets them use their Mercury energy: teaching, all forms of writing, lecturing, number-crunching, communications, and anything detailed and *interesting* to them personally. They dislike too much routine.

Mercury in the eleventh house: With Mercury here, the Gemini Ascendant needs associates that promote the healthy and ongoing development of his or her Mercury function: observant, articulate, open-minded people. He or she also needs life to remain interesting, with plenty of opportunities to keep learning, because the need to feed one's curiosity grows over time with this Mercury placement. Retirement near a university town or other stimulating place would be wise.

Mercury in the twelfth house: Someone with Gemini rising and this placement of Mercury needs to spend some time *observing consciousness* on a regular basis. Meditation works well here, either with a mantra to distract the busy mind, or a meditation upon some external object. This person's inner guru is Mercury, and would suggest an objective study of any interesting form of spirituality, rather than adopting blind faith. Faith is fine, as long as it's preceded by investigation.

ASCENDANT IN CANCER:

The Symbols: This person has come into the world wearing the mask of the Nurturer, the Healer, the Mother, or the Sensitive. Other images for Cancer include the Invisible One, Old Mother Hubbard, the Hobbit, the Rememberer or the Homebody. Less than optimal manifestations of this Ascendant might include the Smother-mother, the Clingy One, the Hypersensitive One, or the Crybaby.

The Style: As with all the water signs, this Ascendant is complex, so we'll spend some extra time here.

Cancer doesn't mean biologically female, but this is the sign of the archetypal feminine, the archetypal Great Goddess, the lunar counterpart to the Leonine Sun God. Think of Cancer as the epitome of "yin" energy, that which is nurturing, receptive, and fertile—and dark, mysterious, inward and unpredictable.

In prehistoric societies now lost in time, before we knew that sex led to babies, we might well have associated the creative function with women, who mysteriously brought forth children from their own flesh and blood. When not bearing children, and before the age of artificial lights, it's likely that women's cycles tended to attune themselves to the approximately twenty-eight day cycle of the Moon.

Until relatively recently in modern astrology, it's been all too easy to dismiss the Moon and the yin territory that it rules, just as it's been all too easy to dismiss the feminine. We would do well to remember that some of the earliest astronomical and astrological records were of the Moon's cycle. The Sun rules the day and is predictably invisible at night. The Moon, who rules the night and the dark, is sometimes visible during the day and sometimes invisible at night. Yin energy is cyclical, too, sometimes dark and sometimes full, just as the Moon waxes and wanes and changes speed. The Moon rules over fertility and birth—*and* over the dark, the night, the real and imaginary creatures who walk there, and the ultimate night of death. As a midwife once told me, "Death is always present at a birth." Perhaps that's one reason, apart from the Moon's phases, why many lunar goddesses have more than one face: maiden, mother, crone.

The Moon rules the high and low tides of our oceans and of our emotional lives, whose karmic imprints we all carry. It rules the body's automatic systems: digestion, endocrine, etc., all the bodily functions that aren't under the conscious control of the mind. The Moon rules the fluids of which our bodies are mostly composed. It rules caves and the chthonic energy associated with them. It rules our ancestors and, I suspect, whatever known or unknown influences they have in our lives.

Just as people with Leo rising wear the Sun God's energy and all it implies of archetypal kingship or even the godhead metaphorically imprinted on their faces, people with Cancer rising carry the full fluctuating weight of the Moon Goddess upon theirs. Someone with a Cancer Ascendant has reached an evolutionary stage where he or she should present a gentle, caring, tender and reflective face to the world. Remember that one of Cancer's traditional symbols is the Crab, a delicate creature with a hard exoskeleton that helps it survive. A person with this Ascendant needs some "shells," some protective mechanisms, some deflector shields. The development of enough discernment to know when to raise the shields and when to lower them is crucial. Otherwise, people with Cancer rising can go through life either inappropriately defended and defensive, or so open and vulnerable that they become co-dependent or are repeatedly hurt and manipulated. Years ago, I heard the astrologer Richard Idemon call *dysfunctional* Cancer "the breast looking for the baby or the baby looking for the breast." To that image I would add "the barnacle:" someone who's shut down behind what could become a PermaShell, usually after bouncing back and forth between those breast-or-baby extremes and not yet integrating them.

People with Cancer rising should face life with imagination, receptivity, the full development of their feeling function and of a rich inner life, and as open a heart as possible consistent with their emotional survival. The fuel is whatever strengthens the feeling function and feeds the imagination and makes it fertile. The terrain is anywhere one must navigate by feeling, intuition and patience rather than by logic.

If the rest of the chart is self-contained and analytical, the Cancer Ascendant is intended to soften this person and help him or her be more aware of the feeling side of life. If the rest of the chart is extraverted and feisty, the Cancer Ascendant is intended to provide some empathy and caution. If the rest of the chart is creative or psychologically oriented, the Cancer Ascendant is intended to help give this person access to deep inner sources of self-awareness. In any case, this rising sign's demeanor should convey the message: "Here is a sensitive, imaginative, empathic and supportive person, who may be quiet or unavailable at the moment, but these still waters run deep."

If no one provided adequate nurturing in the Cancer Ascendant's childhood, this person can become "the baby looking for the breast" and keep searching for someone to play mother, so that he or she can at last be the baby. On the other hand, these people may instead become "the breast looking for the baby" and mother everyone else, all the while ignoring their own needs, perhaps because it's too painful to feel how those needs aren't being met, or perhaps because they're unconsciously hoping to get some mothering back eventually. Another reaction to inadequate early nurturing may be to give up on ever finding any at all, and to withdraw—the "barnacle"—behind the Cancer shell. Such people may be very focused on themselves and on meeting their own needs, while those of others are given short shrift. If the childhood was chaotic, traumatic or dangerous, people with this rising sign can become extremely shy, cautious or self-protective. All of these types would do well to learn about healthy self-nurturing, aided by their own powerful feelings and potentially rich and fertile inner lives. Then it's easier to relate to the outside world from a position of emotional strength and wholeness, rather than need or lack.

The Persona and the Other—the First House/Seventh House Axis:

Someone who *overidentifies* with a Cancer Ascendant can display a few different types of behavior. He or she may find a sick puppy, canine or human. Maybe the "puppy" is weak, shiftless, addicted or needy. Maybe the "puppy" is a powerful solar type whose sickness consists of a great big inflated ego that wants satellites. In either case, the Cancer Ascendant can go into a co-dependent lunar orbit around this person. All conflict is avoided. Everything is forgiven. Such

Cancer Ascendants can hover and fuss and enable, ignoring their own needs and even their sovereignty over their own lives.

Another type of behavior is a timid or even fearful withdrawal from an outside world perceived as too harsh, threatening or demanding. If these Cancer rising people can find some sort of caretaker to aid and abet this withdrawal, they can retreat still further and become very self-indulgent and self-absorbed. Nothing matters more than their feeling-of-the-moment, and they may live in incredible fantasies that they've spun around those feelings. Another type of behavior is a total retreat into the self. These "barnacle" people don't have intimates at all, and only their shell is shown to the outside world.

These examples are of course *not* the typical expressions of healthy Cancer Ascendants. They are only what can happen with *overidentification* with this Ascendant. (Please see Chapter Two for a discussion of the dynamic of overidentification.)

If these extreme expressions of Cancer rising occur, how might the seventh-house Other react? It's possible that the Other may be polarized into various extreme Capricornian responses.

Sometimes the "sick puppy" may decide that he or she now has a sweet deal, and exert control (Capricorn) either by becoming still more dependent, or by assuming the demanding, domineering and emotionally withholding face of Capricorn behavior. Sometimes the "puppy" recovers, becomes a pillar of Capricorn strength and leaves Mommy. If the Cancer Ascendant is the one with a caretaker, the caretaker may gruffly demand that the Cancer rising person start pulling his or her weight, like a Capricorn "straighten up and fly right" lecture. And sadly, no one may try to interact with the "barnacle" at all.

How might these dynamics be avoided?

If you have Cancer rising, *listen* if your partner says, "Good grief, I just have a cold, not the plague. Stop waving tissues under my nose." If you have Cancer rising, *be very suspicious* if your partner wants you to all but give blood for him or her. Ask yourself how and why you've allowed yourself to do virtually nothing but give and to receive little or nothing in return. Ask your partner for reciprocity. If you aren't going to get it, then leave. If you have Cancer rising, *listen* if your partner says, "You had surgery a whole year ago. Your doctor says you've recovered enough to go back to work. Why haven't you?" And *listen* if your partner or someone with a legitimate right to do so is tapping on your shell and requesting that you come out and communicate. Sure, you may have been hurt. Why not say so? You don't have to lower your shields if it's dangerous to do so. But devote some time to figuring out whether it's *really* dangerous, rather than just automatically reinforcing your shields and retreating still further behind them.

If you have Cancer rising, think carefully about what most motivates your choice of partners. Of course you're drawn to Capricornian competence and real-world smarts. In an evolutionary sense, you need such a role model so that you can develop a practical "shell" to help protect you and smooth your own path through life. But are you looking *only* for someone to live your outer life or to direct it for you? Are you trying to turn a person into your shell? Of course you're drawn to Capricornian stability and self-containment. But have you mistaken emotional poverty for depth, and are you trying either to get blood from a stone or to heal this person's "wounds"?

The Vehicle and the Terrain: People with Cancer rising have come into the world with a vehicle—the Cancer Ascendant—that is meant to move through the world as an exercise in the full development of their feeling function and their "yin" side. As the shaman Don Juan Matus in Carlos Castaneda's books says, "For me there is only the traveling on paths that have heart, on any path that may have heart. There I travel, and the only worthwhile challenge is to traverse its full length." Any path with heart is the terrain. The fuel, then, is *enough* *connection to one's heart that one can sense when one has found such a path.*

How can the fuel of such a connection be developed? The inner world of feeling doesn't speak in linear words. Instead, it speaks the native language of the Moon: symbols, memories, feelings and dreams. Therefore, people with this Ascendant may find it helpful to keep a dream journal, to take some time to understand their childhood and their family's psychological patterns, or to work through exercises meant to stimulate creativity, such as those in *The Artist's Way,* by Julia Cameron. The point with creative pursuits isn't so much the creative product itself and the applause it might earn, as with Leo rising. Instead, the point is what the creative process reveals about the Cancer Ascendant's interior life, for the inner world of feeling speaks in our imaginations. It also speaks in what Buddhists call *bodhichitta*, the "awakened" and compassionate heart. In that sense, the fuel and the terrain can, again, be any path with heart. These paths are not always indicated by conventional wisdom or common sense.

Occupational hazards of a Cancer Ascendant include being so bogged down in responding to others' needs or wishes that the paths of one's own heart are left untrodden. People with Cancer rising who aren't stuck in caretaking still run the risk of yielding to the influence of a culture that devalues the yin and lunar side of existence, and simply not granting their inner life enough importance to explore it. Another hazard is responding to life's inevitable bruises by forming so much scar tissue that one no longer follows one's heart or even listens to it. Another hazard is retreating into a rich inner life and refusing to come out.

Staying Comfortable in the Body: If people with Cancer rising are feeling vulnerable and haven't developed any other "shell" or defense mechanism but their physical selves, they may try to hide their bodies with voluminous clothing, or to hide *in* their bodies with obesity or other forms of being unattractive. They should include good care of their bodies in the healthy self-nurturing that is so important to this Ascendant. If they try to stuff down their feelings or starve their emotional or creative lives, they may stuff or starve their bodies, too. It can be interesting for almost everyone to reflect upon how food may have been used as a substitute for love in their families of origin, but since Cancer is traditionally associated with nurturing, food and family, it can be particularly revealing for a Cancer Ascendant to pursue this line of thinking.

Images for a Costume: A doctor's or vet's scrubs. Maternity clothes. Washable, kid-friendly clothes, with apron and cookie jar. A housekeeper's or nanny's uniform. A chef's smock and hat. Gear worn on an anthropology dig. An invisible sign saying "soft absorbent shoulder and listening ear." Nightwear; something to be worn beneath the Moon, complete with dream journal. Anything in which one can hide or be protected.

Images for the Vehicle: A deep-sea submarine with lots of viewing windows, a great galley, comfy beds, and a periscope to see if it's safe to resurface. A mobile kitchen. A "soccer mom" van. A car with tinted windows so no one can see inside. An ambulance or EMT vehicle. A spaceship whose life-support systems and shields never go offline, and a post-sleep-shift room where the crew writes down their dreams undisturbed.

Images for the Terrain: The ocean of feelings and the unconscious, which in dreams often appears as various bodies of water: rivers, streams, pools. The Dreamtime. Moonlit landscapes. Caves. A family therapist's office. A nursery. The historical past. A genealogy conference. A matriarchal culture. Territory where you must navigate by feel, intuition and hunches, not by linear reasoning.

The Ambassador's Host Country—the Moon's House Position:

The Moon's house position is where someone with Cancer rising must be the most willing to heed the emotional tides of his or her life, while not drowning in them. To put it another way, here is where these people must honor their yin energy, but not surrender to it to their own detriment.

Moon in the first house: These people need a particularly juicy expression of Cancer rising; as much as possible, they are meant to wear their hearts on their sleeves. A double dose of safe, non-co-dependent outlets for their nurturing energies can be helpful, as can finding a place to express their vivid imaginations fully and without any specific outcome in mind. Learning how to let the feelings be their *guides* rather than their masters is key here.

Moon in the second house: In order to have healthy self-esteem, this person needs to accept and honor his or her strong emotions. It's helpful to have a safe outlet where those feelings can be expressed and valued by others. The ability to empathize with others is a resource that can be cultivated, as is this person's rich imagination. These people should take care not to invest so much of their self-worth in their ability to nurture that they deplete themselves by devoting too much energy to it.

Moon in the third house: People with Cancer rising and a third house Moon should make sure to meet their strong emotional need for an *interesting* life. They need periodic deep immersion in whatever they find most fascinating at the moment. They do well to develop their ability to communicate, which they can do with great imaginative flair. Care should be taken not to confuse what they're thinking with what they're feeling.

Moon in the fourth house: Cancer Ascendants with the Moon here do well to create a nest-like home that truly nurtures them, as well as anyone living with them. Their homes should make it easy for them to rest, daydream and indulge in flights of fancy. They do well to reflect upon their early lives, in order to see where they may have identified with either a parent's or with their whole families' emotional lives more than was helpful for them.

Moon in the fifth house: These people need to express themselves creatively, to make room for the whimsical and the spontaneous in their lives. Relationships that can become important to them will have a tender, imaginative, lunar quality to their early stages. They need to allow themselves to have fun, or their inner lives won't be fed. Care should be taken not to focus so much on their children's or partners' recreation that they have no fun themselves.

Moon in the sixth house: With the Moon here, these people have an emotional need to become competent at some sort of yin, lunar craft or skill. This does not mean they have an emotional need to adopt every orphaned responsibility they spot looking for a home. They should focus on assuming responsibilities that they enjoy, and that may well involve imagination and inner work as well as empathy, reflective listening and caring.

Moon in the seventh house: With the Moon here, this person benefits from relationships where the nurturing is as mutual and reciprocal as possible. Friends and partners should be caring, gentle and intuitive. This person should be mindful not to flip back and forth between overnurturing and undernurturing the partner, and not to project his or her own imagination and inner life onto the partner and claim none for his or her own.

Moon in the eighth house: With the Moon here, this person's natural mate, and those who make the deepest psychological impact on him or her, should be emotionally fluent people with a strong feminine side and great tenderness. Care should be taken to choose a mate whose lunar function is well balanced, rather than labile and needy. Although there's an emotional need here to process deep psychological material, care should be taken not to do so obsessively.

Moon in the ninth house: With Cancer rising and the Moon in the ninth house, this person's guiding star is his or her Moon. Developing a strong, healthy expression of one's lunar energies, and following one's heart, become all the more important. This lunar expression shouldn't be too moody, self-indulgent or unmoored from reason, or these people run the risk of turning their feelings into their god, and expecting everyone else to worship at that altar too.

Moon in the tenth house: People with Cancer rising and this Moon placement should create a vocation or avocation that lets them fully use their sensitive lunar energies and be recognized for them. They should avoid accepting any caretaking job that comes down the pike, and aim instead for something that both speaks to their hearts and lets them express their hearts.

Moon in the eleventh house: With the Moon here, a Cancer Ascendant has an emotional need for goals and associates that nourish the healthy blooming of his or her lunar function. These people are happiest when they've brought a cherished plan to fruition, however great or small. Their natural allies are soulful, heart-centered people with equally yin goals. Care should be taken not to nurture others' projects at the expense of their own.

Moon in the twelfth house: With Cancer rising and the Moon here, this person has an emotional need to dedicate some regular time to daily meditation or some other form of quiet, devotional inner work. Their "inner guru" is their Moon, who in this case advises that they investigate the nature of their feelings and how those feelings relate to their consciousness or spirit.

ASCENDANT IN LEO:

The Symbols: This person has come into the world wearing the mask of the Performer, the King or Queen, the Aristocrat or the Clown. Other images for Leo include the Lion, the Star, the Golden Boy or Girl, or the Childlike One. Lower level manifestations of this sign's energy might be the Dictator, the Prima Donna, the Narcissist or the Spoiled Brat.

The Style: This Ascendant is complex, so we'll spend some extra time here.

This man or woman has reached an evolutionary stage where he or she must present a positive, playful, creative and generous face to the world. Considerable presence may accompany this rising sign, whether the person is aware of it or not. This is the mask of *the Sun God or Goddess*, and it radiates—and should radiate—a lot of powerfully charismatic solar energy. I've often wished that someone would do a Kirlian photography study of the auras of the different rising signs. I suspect that, all other things being equal, the aura of a Leo Ascendant in good health simply emanates more sheer energy that's perceptible from a greater distance than the auras of the other Ascendants.

Kingship in ancient cultures was often intermingled or confused with the godhead. In other words, sovereigns in those cultures often either claimed to be God or one of the gods, or accepted their people's projection of the godhead upon them. There was an ancient belief that, just as God is creative and nourishes the land, when the sovereign is healthy, flourishing and creative, so is the country. (The reverse could also be believed, that if the ruler was ill, the land would suffer too.) Think of the benevolent sovereign, rewarding the knights, blessing the people, and inspiring confidence partly through the sheer pageantry of his or her display.

People with Leo rising can still seem touched with this almost sacred power and ability to inspire reverence, loyalty and even awe. Moreover, having Leo rising automatically turns up the volume on one's Sun, regardless of its placement in the signs. It's as if a Leo Ascendant has a double dose of solar energy: one from the Leo Ascendant and one from the way that Ascendant strengthens that person's Sun. It's important for someone with Leo rising to use this energy wisely, rather than squander it with arrogance or ego-inflation.

If the rest of the chart is less vivid or more timid, the Leo Ascendant may be difficult to integrate, yet it's intended not only to protect the rest of the chart but also to express it, to help it be seen and heard. If the rest of the chart is equally colorful, the Leo Ascendant is intended to express it, to dress it up, show it off and get it noticed. For both shrinking violets and extraverts, this rising sign's demeanor should convey: "Here is a prince among men or a princess among women, a generous, creative person who isn't afraid to take up space, who treats others with largesse. *Noblesse oblige . . .* "

If family members didn't affirm the Leo Ascendant during childhood, constantly criticized him or her, or felt they had to crush that aura of solar presence, a more retiring person may hesitate to do the very "shining" that's so important to this rising sign. A stronger person may present a false self in order to get the family's praise, or give up on the family and try for praise elsewhere, sometimes with flamboyant "acting out" behavior. If the family spoiled a Leo rising child, he or she can continue to expect star treatment. All of these types can have felt that any attention was better than none, sometimes with disastrous results. All of them need somewhere to shine, to give of themselves *and* to be appreciated for it, in order to feel grounded.

The Persona and the Other—the First House/Seventh House Axis:

Someone who *overidentifies* with a Leo Ascendant appears to have a tremendous "superiority complex." These people can act as if they think they're kings or gods, insisting on their own way at all costs, and wanting adoration and preferential treatment. Prima donnas, they have to be the center of attention and can react badly if anyone else is. They can be overbearing and imperious. They are always "on," always trying to impress everyone. They can enthrall others for a while, but as people get tired of their bombast and self-centeredness, they may need an ever-changing audience of new admirers.

If what people with a Leo Ascendant present for praise and admiration is a false self, their act can become very strained—and so can they; such an act is exhausting to maintain. Sadly, all this aggrandizement, whether of the true self or the false, often drives away the very support, belonging and recognition that Leo rising seeks. Then the Leo Ascendant may try all the harder, and a vicious cycle can be set into motion.

These behaviors are of course *not* the typical expression of a healthy Leo Ascendant. They are only what *may* happen with *overidentification* with this rising sign. (Please see Chapter Two for a discussion of the dynamic of overidentification in this context.)

How might the seventh-house Other react to such extreme behavior? It's possible that the Other might be polarized into various Aquarian responses.

One obvious Aquarian response is rebellion. "You think you're the King? Forget it. If you don't quit trying to boss me around, I'm outta here." A weaker personality may not leave, but may fight back by passive aggression, detachment and withdrawal, or by reflexively contradicting everything Leo rising says, right or wrong. Another response might be to mock the Leo Ascendant, to point out, gleefully, wherever and whenever the Emperor has no clothes. A disrespected Leo Ascendant can feel very hurt or insulted, and typically does not take criticism or mockery lying down.

How might this dynamic be avoided? If you have Leo rising, *listen* if your partner says, "Will you please stop unilaterally decreeing things? Could we have a conversation and make a decision together?" *Listen* if your partner says, "I know you may not have been seen and appreciated for yourself when you were growing up—but your leftover hunger for attention is really causing you problems today, so it's causing us problems too. May I give you some examples?" Or if your partner says, "It's not all about you! I praise you a lot; how about praising me sometimes?"

If you have Leo rising, think carefully about what most influences your choice of mate. Of course you're drawn to Aquarian independence. In an evolutionary sense, you need Aquarius energy to model for you how to be completely yourself, and not to present a false self calculated to get maximum notice. But are you harboring any dim, secret feeling that if you can just get *this* free spirit drawn into your solar orbit, it'll prove you're *really* someone special? Of course you like Aquarian originality. But are you projecting your own very real creativity onto someone else rather than living it yourself, because it's too scary to risk failure or criticism?

The Vehicle and the Terrain: Someone with this rising sign has arrived on the planet with a vehicle—the Leo Ascendant—that is meant to move through life as a kind of exercise in the power of positive thinking or attitude adjustment. The attitude should be one of joy, of comfort in the body and on the planet, and of a playful, generative warmth that reaches out to others, where the Leo "crown" is worn lightly.

Think of the benevolent sovereign mentioned a few paragraphs ago. I know a woman who gave her well-intentioned but imperious and rather formal mother a cushion embroidered with the words, "It's *good* to be Queen." The woman's friends had expressed concerns that the gift might cause offense. Far from it: the mother was a woman who got her own joke. She laughed, then melted. Beaming, she hugged the cushion, and spent weeks showing it off to her many visitors—her "court." She still displays it prominently on her sofa.

The terrain is anywhere the Leo Ascendant can shine and even "rule." Again, consider how ancient cultures often associated the Sun with God. In most cultures, at least one God, usually the main one, is a creator-God. People with this rising sign needs to say "yes" to life, to trust others, to trust themselves, and to trust God if that lies within their belief system. This Leonine attitude of acceptance, joy and generosity of spirit is far easier to maintain if this Ascendant "imitates God" *by being creative and being appreciated for it.*

The terrain, therefore, is also anywhere the Leo Ascendant can create something "shiny" and share it with others. The experiential fuel this Leo vehicle needs can be dramatic and colorful, and should involve the risk of having one's creative core seen by an audience. The terrain it should cover is anywhere that the driver can enjoy being noticed and applauded for sharing that solar "star quality."

Occupational hazards of a Leo Ascendant include a tendency toward acting like a tyrant instead of a good king or queen. Another risk can be some form of merely making noise to get noticed, instead of giving something from one's core. Such behavior can include pouring so much energy into that starry surface that the rest of one's life and creative output can suffer—I've had clients with Leo rising who would not venture outside their own houses if they'd gained weight or sprouted a pimple. People with this Ascendant may not *feel* as confident as they can *appear,* and sometimes those appearances can work against their need for appreciation. If there's been too much painfully negative feedback for a Leo Ascendant's creative efforts or personal self-expression, he or she may shut down in order not to risk such criticism again, and thereby lose access to a major part of the terrain these people so need to cross in this lifetime. Therefore, their prospective audiences should be chosen carefully at first, because some people are simply not capable of giving positive feedback to anyone.

Staying Comfortable in the Body: Like it or not, Leo rising's solar aura tends to make an impression and get noticed. Many people with this Ascendant sense this dynamic and become very focused on their appearance. Wanting to look reasonably good for one's age can be an expression of healthy self-respect. However, moving into the gym and funding a plastic surgeon's Bermuda mansion may have more to do with feeling a lack of recognition for one's *true* self, and trying to get recognition for one's physical self instead. Keeping the body healthy enough to enjoy life and creativity might be one good compromise.

Images for a Costume: A king's or queen's robes, crown and scepter. A clown's costume. Anything the stars might wear on Oscar night. High-end, high-fashion clothing. Formal wear. Flashy, glitzy, look-at-me clothing. Something the "uppah clawsses" might wear. A lion's pelt, mane and roar. Stage makeup. "Fine feathers."

Images for the Vehicle: A stretch limo. A Jaguar. A very red, very shiny convertible. A sleek, classic, high-end sedan: a Mercedes, a Rolls-Royce. An open car in which royalty rides to wave to the masses. A rock and roll band's tour bus. Jean-Luc Picard's chair on the bridge of the Enterprise. Something in which to carry creative supplies. Anything in which to see and be seen.

Images for the Terrain: A country where this person rules, preferably as *a benevolent and loved* sovereign, and where everyone thrives on ceremony. A stage on which to perform, preferably for an appreciative audience. Opening night. A film set. A red carpet. The Academy Awards or their equivalent. Territory one has to navigate by using the sheer force of one's presence.

The Ambassador's Host Country—The Sun's House Position:
   Since the Sun rules Leo, someone with Leo rising should aim for a particularly powerful expression of his or her Sun, which gains even more importance than usual as both the ego-function and sanity (Sun), and as the ruler of the Ascendant. The Sun's house position is where this person really needs to shine.
Sun in the first house: This person needs a particularly radiant expression of Leo rising, full of presence, warmth, a regal quality and a touch of theater—the persona should be *enjoyed*. A double dose of experiences such as creativity and performance might be indicated, and it's most helpful if they earn genuine appreciation. If this person overdoes the Ascendant, he or she could become too egocentric and seek notoriety for its own sake, rather than recognition for authentic self-expression.

Sun in the second house: In order to have healthy self-esteem, a Leo Ascendant with the Sun here needs to develop a well-integrated ego (Sun) with good boundaries and a certain expressive flair. It's bolstering for these people to develop a good sense of their inner resources and talents. Care should be taken not to develop an exaggerated notion of their own importance as a compensation for any tendencies toward an inferiority complex.

Sun in the third house: People with Leo rising and a third house Sun need to enjoy exercising their functions of perception and communication, preferably with appreciative responses from others. They also need to nourish their curiosity, avoid prejudice and remain open to new information. They do well to avoid rationalizations that merely feed the ego and lessen their objectivity.

Sun in the fourth house: Leo Ascendants with the Sun here do well to create a home where they feel like the proud holder of the best traditions of their roots. Home should seem like a palace fit to shelter their "royal blood." They also do well to examine their early lives and consider whether they're granting either a strong parent or their entire clan too much power and influence over their own psyches.

Sun in the fifth house: These people need a creative outlet that they enjoy, preferably one that includes an audience of any size. They do well to experience a wide range of the various pleasures life can offer, rather than getting stuck on just one or two. They particularly enjoy the early stages of relating. Care should be taken not to avoid responsibilities, and not to terminate relationships the instant the first bloom is off the rose.

Sun in the sixth house: With the Sun here, finding a craft at which to excel is extremely important. These people need meaningful work and/or mentoring into which they can pour themselves and with which they can identify. Work that earns them personal recognition would be a plus. Care should be taken not to become a workaholic or an office tyrant.

Sun in the seventh house: With the Sun here, this person benefits from relationships where he or she feels fully seen and fully met. Friends and partners should have a strong sense of their own identity, and creativity or a certain colorful presence on their part is a plus. Care should be taken not to go into orbit around such partners' strong solar energy. Instead, a Leo Ascendant can learn from these people how to develop his or her own solar strengths.

Sun in the eighth house: With the Sun here, this person's natural mate, and the people who make the deepest psychological impact on him or her, should be charismatic with lots of "star" quality. Care should be taken to choose a mate whose solar function is well-balanced and well-integrated, rather than self-centered and overbearing. Although these Leo Ascendants can be psychologically oriented and intense, they should be mindful of not overdramatizing their own issues.

Sun in the ninth house: With Leo rising and the Sun in the ninth house, this person's guiding star is his or her Sun. Developing a strong and healthy expression of one's solar energies, and living according to one's principles, are both essential. Yet this solar expression shouldn't be conceited or overblown, or these people run the risk of making self-worship their religion, and of trying to convert others to that belief. "Know yourself; don't glorify yourself" might be their motto.

Sun in the tenth house: People with Leo rising and this Sun placement should create a vocation or avocation that lets them fully employ the energies of their Sun sign and be personally recognized for it. That can mean breaking some eggs to make the proverbial omelet, although it doesn't have to mean being domineering. They should avoid jobs that have status but don't make them feel, "I can't believe I'm getting paid to do something I love so much!"

Sun in the eleventh house: With the Sun here, a Leo Ascendant needs goals and associates that encourage and applaud the healthy flourishing of his or her solar function. Making plans and following through on them are essential. Cultivating groups of sane and centered allies would be helpful. These Leo Ascendants should avoid overidentifying with any one group, however, and should resist peer pressure to pursue goals that lack appeal for them personally.

Sun in the twelfth house: With Leo rising and the Sun here, this person should devote some regular time to daily meditation or some other form of quiet, contemplative inner work. Their "inner guru" is the Sun, who in this case advises that they investigate the nature of the ego (the Sun) in the metaphysical sense. That doesn't mean either glorifying or trying to eradicate the ego; it means exploring how the ego relates to consciousness.

ASCENDANT IN VIRGO:

The Symbols: This person has come into the world wearing the mask of the Craftsperson, the Analyst, the Worker, the Details Person or the Growth Ninja. Other images for Virgo rising include the Perfectionist, the Servant, the Critic, the Apprentice or the Health Nut. Less than optimal manifestations of this Ascendant might include the Faultfinder, the Drudge, the Slave, the Hypochondriac or the Self-Saboteur. (Apologies if some of these terms are unwieldy, but simpler ones wouldn't convey their full meaning.)

The Style: This Ascendant's dynamics are sufficiently complicated that we'll spend some extra time here.

This man or woman has reached an evolutionary stage where he or she should present a practical, can-do, detail-oriented, humble but not servile face to the world. The development of honest self-appraisal and a dedication to self-improvement are essential. Life should be confronted with honesty, humility, self-awareness, and a bedrock decision *to like oneself enough both to allow oneself to grow, and to claim the right, fulfilling work.*

If the rest of the chart is fiery, passionate and demonstrative, the Virgo Ascendant is intended to help these people not get too full of themselves. If the rest of the chart is highly inward and emotional, this Ascendant is intended to help this person use meaningful work as a tonic to prevent too much self-absorption. If the rest of the chart is serious and analytical, the Virgo Ascendant is intended to develop and express those qualities. In any case, this rising sign's demeanor should convey the message: "Here is someone who's mastered a craft or a skill and can use it in a common-sensical, helpful way. Here is someone with a keen eye for detail, but even though he notices all the flaws in everything around him, he has enough healthy self-esteem not to need to pump himself up by putting others down all the time."

In childhood, these people were extremely sensitive to any real or implied criticism from their family or their environment in general. Meanwhile, all kids need toilet training, get sick, spill milk, and make messes and mistakes; that just goes with being a kid. But if the Virgo Ascendant's family was unreasonably picky, squeamish or punitive about such matters, a more sensitive person can have decided there was *something wrong with him or her*, and not see that it was his or her *behavior* that bothered a family member. Virgo Ascendants may internalize such decisions about themselves as low self-esteem. As adults, this dynamic, if unexamined, may continue, and Virgo Ascendants may try all the harder to be perfect, out of fear of continued criticism and punishment that was all out of proportion to the "offense." A hardier person with Virgo rising, who learned to shut out negative feedback in order to survive childhood, can become defensive about any and all criticism, no matter how appropriate or constructive and no matter what the source. Both types do well to turn that analytical Virgoan eye to their own upbringing. Perhaps, because this Mercury-ruled Ascendant benefits from lots of communication, they might compare their upbringing to that of other people, to help them recognize where their own family's standards, expectations and reactions might have been extreme. Then it will be easier for the

Virgo Ascendant to stop applying those unrealistic standards either to themselves or to others.

The Persona and the Other—the First House/Seventh House Axis:

Someone who *overidentifies* with a Virgo Ascendant can display a few different types of behavior.

A person who overidentifies with a Virgo Ascendant and has low self-esteem may project the self-assessing function outward some or all of the time, because it's too painful to apply it to himself or herself. In that event, this rising sign can become extremely critical. Nothing is ever good enough. No one else is ever good enough, either, and the Virgo Ascendant's partner may bear the brunt of his or her criticism. A related phenomenon can be an effort to make and keep one's work, house or other surroundings *perfect*. Change and entropy are inescapable and powerful forces, so such efforts are doomed to fail, which may reduce this rising sign to trying even harder to resist those forces. The concept that "sometimes perfect is the enemy of good enough" simply isn't on such a person's radar screen, so projects may never be completed or partners may be alienated in an anxious and tunnel-visioned pursuit of an impossible ideal.

A person who overidentifies with a Virgo Ascendant and hasn't achieved personally fulfilling work may extend that critical function to his or her office, boss, co-workers, clients and customers, not to mention the state of the economy or the state of the government. Their list of flaws and flawed people and institutions seems endless.

Meanwhile, the only people who appear to escape any blame for the Virgo Ascendants' not having found the right work, the right house, the right partner, etc., are the Virgo Ascendants themselves—when they may well be their own worst enemies. People who feel guilty often punish themselves. Driving all the critical behavior I've described in the last few paragraphs can be a conscious or unconscious *guilt over not being perfect.* A person dealing with such an issue can not only project it outward rather than feel it inwardly, but can also punish himself *with his behavior.* He abuses his health with substances or overwork. She fails to get the necessary credentials for work she was born to do, but can't be hired to do without those credentials. He runs late for an important job interview or misses it altogether. Why? Because he's trying to punish himself for not being perfect, trying to wipe out the flawed human being he believes himself to be.

These examples are of course *not* the typical expressions of healthy Virgo Ascendants. They are only what can happen with *overidentification* with this Ascendant. (Please see Chapter Two for a discussion of the dynamic of overidentification.)

If these extreme expressions of Virgo rising occur, how might the seventh-house Other react? It's possible that the Other may be polarized into various extreme Piscean responses.

"It's hopeless trying to satisfy you, so I'll just let things slide. Since you're going to nitpick every detail anyway, why should I bother to pay attention to anything?" Here's Piscean energy as the disorganized flake.

"If all *you're* going to do is criticize and judge, then all *I'm* going to do is approve and forgive and include." Here's the Piscean lack of boundaries and discrimination.

"If you're going to be such a workaholic, do I even need a job? Besides, you're so critical I'm starting to lose confidence that I could do anything right." Here's Piscean learned helplessness.

"I'm sick of your constant fault-finding. I'm leaving." This person may either leave the relationship or withdraw into various escapist (Piscean) behaviors.

If any of the above dynamics go to extremes, the Virgo Ascendant can become miffed at "being forced" to micromanage the Other, and a vicious circle can be exacerbated. How might such scenarios be avoided?

If you have Virgo rising, *listen* if your partner says, "Do you think I ever do anything *right*? It'd be nice to get some praise once in a while instead of nothing but criticism." Let go of the details of who said what when, and give your partner some praise.

Listen if your partner says: "No matter what anyone's done, you immediately point out something wrong with it. It hurts people's feelings and alienates them and makes you look impossible to please." Or if your partner says, "If you just felt better about yourself, you might not have to cut other people down all the time." Try starting with thanks for everything someone did well, and you're far more likely to be heard if you *must* add some unavoidable criticism.

Listen if your partner says, "Should I wash behind my ears, too?" No one needs breathing lessons. *Listen* when your partner says, "You're miserable at work, but that's not the only job in the world. Why not investigate doing something you'd like more?" Above all, don't dismiss that last question out of hand. The right work can be almost miraculously helpful to your ability to feel centered.

If you have Virgo rising, think carefully about what most influences your choice of partner. First of all, you may actually be in a relationship with a helpless, out-to-lunch, escapist flake who refuses to acknowledge that he or she is living in the same space/time continuum as the rest of the planet. But if that's the case, and you've objected and been patient but your partner hasn't changed, then why are you still there? Maybe it's because you don't feel that you deserve any better. Healthy self-esteem is crucial for this Ascendant.

Of course you're drawn to Piscean warmth and compassion. In an evolutionary sense, you can benefit from careful observation of this person's capacity for inclusiveness, forgiveness and tolerance. But are you too dependent on your partner's ability to smooth all the feathers that your critical faculty may have ruffled? Of course you find the Piscean ability to let little things go appealing. But are you unconsciously looking for someone else to focus on, so that micromanaging his or her life becomes a way for you to avoid working on yourself? Of course you're drawn to Piscean ethereality and the Piscean sense of something larger than our own egos at work in our lives. But are you letting your partner carry all that energy for you, while you play the role of the judgmental skeptic? Once in a while we all need to stop analyzing life, accept its mysterious elements, and just let go and live it.

The Vehicle and the Terrain: A person with Virgo rising arrived on the planet with a vehicle—the Virgo Ascendant—which is meant to move through life as an exercise in personal growth, while feeling *whole* rather than perfect. To that end, the Virgo vehicle has some specialized equipment. People with this rising sign have a clear, detailed picture of exactly who they are, good points and faults alike. They also have just as comprehensive a picture of who they could be, if they'd eradicated all those faults. The distance between those two pictures can either depress them and make them so critical that they can be self-sabotaging or even self-destructive—or it can inspire them to weed out their faults and emphasize their strengths.

People with this Ascendant need two kinds of fuel. One kind is absolute self-acceptance and positive self-regard, not the sort of complacency that sees no need for growth, and not self-flagellation because they're not perfect. The other kind of fuel is competence or even excellence at a personally meaningful skill. The terrain, then, is anywhere the Virgo Ascendant can grow without shame or shaming, and anywhere he or she can enjoy working.

These people do well to consider how their upbringing may have affected their self-esteem, to learn what helps build their self-regard now, and to spend some time at those activities on a regular basis, at work or outside the office or both. They also do well to claim fulfilling work. I emphasize this point because I've seen finding the right job all but work magic overnight in the lives and the outlooks of my Virgo rising clients. Unfortunately, it's all too easy for them to find the wrong work. Why? Because of a possible lack of self-esteem that may make them feel they don't deserve a satisfying job, or may contribute to their failure to qualify for it. And also because this Ascendant needs to feel useful, so Virgo rising people can be walking targets for any responsibility looking for a taker. Although none of us feel thrilled with our jobs *all* the time, the goal is for someone with a Virgo Ascendant to find a job that he or she fundamentally likes and finds rewarding, something that emphasizes one of his or her strengths. If people with Virgo rising are independently wealthy and don't need to work, the same logic applies: they should find a skill or a craft they enjoy doing well, and opportunities to use it.

How to find the right work? One answer comes from the field of employment counseling. If you have Virgo rising, figure out what you feel best about having accomplished over the course of your life. Make a list of perhaps two dozen items, and don't limit them to just what you've done at work. Maybe you feel great about having rescued and adopted your dog, or having introduced two friends who now have a good marriage. What did you do to accomplish these things? How did you do it? Why did it make you feel satisfied? Narrow the list to the top six or so items, then ask yourself, "What sort of job could a person with these skills do well?" Ask all of your friends that question. Consider finding a couple of good employment counselors—check their references—and asking them too.

Occupational hazards of this rising sign have been pretty well covered in this section but are worth repeating here. Virgo rising's risks include burnout, if the right or wrong employment isn't tempered with enough down time or vacation time. Without the proper work, this person can feel like an increasingly resentful drudge at even a well-paid and prestigious job. Another hazard can be taking on too much responsibility for a partner or family members, who may come to expect this behavior and grow increasingly irresponsible themselves. People with this Ascendant may criticize themselves or others ruthlessly, eventually driving people away.

Staying Comfortable in the Body: If a Virgo Ascendant hasn't developed healthy self-esteem, and hasn't realized that wholeness is a better goal than perfection, then that search for perfection can be turned toward the body, or the body can be punished for not being ideal. Because Virgo is an Earth sign, the focus is more likely to be on perfecting the body's health and functioning than its looks, although they can come in for scrutiny too. Virgo Ascendants feel more centered if they feel healthy, and there's nothing wrong with that attitude in and of itself. It's helpful for a Virgo rising person to accept that even if there were such a thing as perfect health, it wouldn't last forever. With such an attitude, it's easier to devote a *reasonable* amount of time, money, exercise and even research—this is a Mercury-ruled sign—to one's physical health. If the effort applied to attaining good health doesn't in reality hurt one's body, or detract from one's peace of mind, relationships, solvency or job, then it's probably reasonable.

Images for a Costume: Work clothes, regardless of the job. An accountant's eyeshade, with a green desk lamp, a pocket protector, some four-color pens and quadrilled paper. A lab coat. A calculator and a slide rule. Neat, practical garments. Comfortable, serviceable and easily cleaned clothes, with plenty of pockets and a PDA with extra batteries.

Images for the Vehicle: A well-equipped sedan with a high reliability rating, receipts for any work ever done on it, and a well-thumbed manual. Any vehicle used at or for work, and/or one that carries a toolbox, preferably including a Swiss Army knife with every available attachment. If this person's trying to bolster self-esteem, it may be some form of status car. If this person has low self-esteem, it may be some version of a rust bucket.

Images for the Terrain: The office, garage, shop, lab, etc. A training school or practicum of any kind. An internship for one's ideal job. A personal growth seminar. The self-help aisle of the bookstore. Anywhere one has to navigate by an ability to juggle details and be precise. Any territory that can be successfully navigated only by people with healthy self-worth and a skill they enjoy using.

The Ambassador's Host Country—Mercury's House Position:
    Mercury's house position is where someone with Virgo rising most needs to work on self-acceptance and self-improvement, without getting bogged down in too many details. Mercury's house position may also give clues about what sort of meaningful skills this person possesses.

Mercury in the first house: This person needs a particularly alert expression of Virgo rising, with all the evaluative faculties working at maximum. A double dose of time and attention spent perfecting a craft or an expertise can help this person grow, and unconditional self-acceptance is essential. People who overdo this placement risk overwork, and/or being so self-critical that they don't allow themselves to grow.

Mercury in the second house: With Mercury here, this person's critical skills can help him or her with self-esteem. This astrological signature refers to developing confidence in one's practical intelligence—a modern version of living by one's wits. However, care should be taken not to make one's problem-solving abilities the only measure of self-worth. Improving the ability to work with both inner and material resources is important.

Mercury in the third house: Someone with Virgo rising and Mercury in the third house needs to focus on the curious and discriminating side of this Ascendant. These people need a regular diet of interesting new experiences to evaluate and discuss. The ongoing improvement of their analytical, observational and communicative skills is particularly important.

Mercury in the fourth house: These people benefit from a home environment that promotes an active life of the mind, not just in a narrow intellectual sense. Home should be a place where study and practice of a skill or craft can readily happen. It's helpful to spend some time understanding how the family system, particularly a Mercurial parent, affected this person's attitudes toward learning, work and responsibility.

Mercury in the fifth house: A Virgo Ascendant with a fifth house Mercury needs to enjoy using his or her mind. Acquiring new skills that employ the thinking function can be particularly pleasant for these people. A hint that a new relationship could last and be important is that the partner is articulate and observant, and can maintain a good mental rapport. Care should be taken not to become so addicted to mental stimulation that anything routine becomes distasteful.

Mercury in the sixth house: People with Virgo rising and this Mercury placement should seek meaningful work that's the opposite of boring for them. A craft that uses the Mercurial skills of perceiving and juggling details, or even of working with one's hands, would be helpful. Mentors and protegés should be chosen with an eye for their curiosity and articulateness.

Mercury in the seventh house: With Mercury here, this person benefits from relationships (partnerships, friendships) with inquisitive and observant people. Improving one's ability to maintain a searching intimate dialog is important. Ideally, the partner is analytical and discriminating but not overly critical, and recognizes and encourages the Virgo Ascendant's own intelligence and perceptions.

Mercury in the eighth house: A Virgo Ascendant with this Mercury placement needs to feel that the bond with a mate involves a capacity for deep conversation about such frequently taboo subjects as sexuality, death, the occult, and the psychological material of which nightmares are made. Such conversations should involve frankness, soul-searching and a minimum of criticism.

Mercury in the ninth house: The philosophy of life that works best for this person might be "Use your head" or "Think it through." Analysis, forethought and communication are just as important as leading an interesting life with plenty of chewy intellectual food. Failing to spot patterns and learn from them could make life feel meaningless.

Mercury in the tenth house: People with Virgo rising and this Mercury placement do well to have a career or avocation that lets them use their Mercury energy in a detailed and judicious way: research; the more comprehensive and technical forms of writing and communication; analysis; a craft that requires painstaking hand-and-eye-coordination, etc. Their work needs to fascinate them rather than bore or overwhelm them.

Mercury in the eleventh house: With Mercury here, the Virgo Ascendant needs associates who promote the ongoing healthy development of his or her Mercury function—reflective, intelligent, articulate people. A Virgo Ascendant with this Mercury placement does well to have long term goals that involve learning, communicating, and satisfying curiosities, because his or her need for all of the above will grow over time.

Mercury in the twelfth house: Someone with Virgo rising and this Mercury placement needs to spend some time doing inner work on a regular and thoughtful basis. Meditation can work well here; blind credulousness does not. This person's "inner guru" is Mercury, and such a guru would counsel investigation of and analytical conversation about spiritual interests and practices.

ASCENDANT IN LIBRA:

The Symbols: This person has come into the world wearing the mask of the Artist, Lover, Counselor, or Peacemaker. Other images for Libra rising include the Negotiator, Diplomat, Aesthetic One or

Moderator. Less than optimal manifestations of this Ascendant might include the Fence-Sitter, Co-Dependent One, Conflict-Avoider, or Indecisive One.

The Style: This man or woman has reached an evolutionary stage where he or she should present a gracious, civilized, charming face to the world. The development of empathy, excellent social skills and a strong aesthetic sense is important. Life should be met with a sincere attempt to achieve and maintain both inner equilibrium, and equilibrium between the self and the surrounding environment, to which Libra rising is extremely sensitive. If the rest of the chart is more rough-and-ready, the Libran Ascendant is intended to soften this person and make his or her self-presentation more palatable to others. If the rest of the chart is timid and reflective, the Libran Ascendant is intended to draw this person into much-needed contact with others. If the rest of the chart is detached and analytical, the Libran Ascendant is intended to help this person develop more emotional intelligence. In any case, this rising sign's demeanor should convey the message: "Here is a warm, fair-minded, aesthetically sensitive person who's genuinely interested in others."

In childhood, people with Libra rising were hyper-aware of their environment, all their family members, and anyone else who was close to them. Because of Libra's drive for equilibrium, they may have attempted to placate and pacify any upset relatives, even if being the peacemaker came at their own expense. More fragile or less self-aware adults with this Ascendant may still blame themselves for any conflicts, and turn themselves inside out in order to be what they think their friends and partners want. Stronger people with Libra rising may still find any sort of disagreement extremely disturbing, and avoid even necessary conflicts more than is good for them. Both types may sometimes benefit from taking some deep calming breaths and remembering that *their needs are just as important as the needs of others*, not more so and not less so.

The Persona and the Other—the First House/Seventh House Axis:

This Ascendant's typical capacity for sweetness, diplomacy, adaptability, and genuine interest in others tends to get a lot of appreciative responses from other people. Libra rising thrives when others feel warmly connected to him or her, which reinforces all the accomodating Libran behavior which helped create that feeling in the first place. Therefore, unless the rest of the chart is that of a fire-breathing snake-eater, people with Libra rising are probably more likely to overidentify with their Ascendants than the rest of us are to overidentify with ours. However, since Libra is an Air sign, Libran Ascendants can be just as adept at analyzing (Air) their own behavior as they can be at figuring out how to please others, and can readily learn to recognize when they get caught up in this dynamic.

People who *overidentify* with their Libran Ascendants can display a few different types of behavior. They may become so focused on pleasing others that they ignore their own desires. If that pattern goes to extremes, they may even lose touch with their own needs, and can start to feel as if they've disappeared into their partners, families or friends. Metaphorically speaking, if all a Libran Ascendant does is anticipate and mirror others' wishes, tastes and whimsies, he or she can get lost in that mirror. Should that happen, much time, effort and soul-searching may be necessary for the Libran Ascendant to put aside others' expectations, climb out of the mirror and figure out what he or she really wants.

A related behavior can be going to any lengths to avoid conflict. Bending over backwards for too long is exhausting, not calming, and doesn't lead to the equilibrium that Libra rising seeks. Moreover, no one can please everyone all the time no matter how hard he or she tries, because people have very different and often conflicting needs.

Another possible manifestation of overidentification with a Libran Ascendant can be too much focus on appearances, until etiquette, style, appropriateness and "niceness" may all become a mannered formality that can squeeze the life and vitality out of the Libran Ascendant and threaten to squelch anyone in his or her orbit. Could you maintain true intimacy in all its gritty depths with someone who demanded that you were both on your very best behavior *all the time?* How would you ever know what he or she was really thinking and feeling?

These examples are of course *not* the typical expressions of healthy Libran Ascendants. They are only what can happen with *overidentification* with this Ascendant. (Please see Chapter Two for a discussion of the dynamic of overidentification.)

If these extreme expressions of Libra rising occur, how might the seventh-house Other react? It's possible that the Other may be polarized into various extreme Arian responses.

How would you feel if you'd been confined in formal wear, uncomfortable shoes and white gloves all evening, nibbling on delicate *hors d'oeuvres* while minding your manners and your grammar? You'd probably want to do something like go home, put on sneakers and sweats, chow down on a pizza in the living room, and catch up with your buddies who don't mind hearing an occasional four-letter word. That's more or less how the Other can react if faced with the Miss Manners version of an overdeveloped Libran Ascendant. The more prim and proper the Libran Ascendant, the more the Other can start fighting a bizarre and uncharacteristic urge to hurtle a television set through the hotel window . . .

If the Libran Ascendant persists in too much mirroring of the Other's needs, then there are no checks and balances on the Other's behavior, and the Other can take merciless advantage of the Libra rising person and even descend into bullying. If you don't set boundaries with a bully, what do you get? The bullying escalates. If the Libran Ascendant is too focused on avoiding disagreement and trying to meet everyone's needs, the Other can expect the Libran Ascendant to keep right on jumping through still more hoops, and never to have any needs of his or her own. If one day the Libra rising person becomes so appalled at this "barbaric treatment" that she starts to assert herself, disagree and state her own needs, the Other can react with angry bewilderment: "You've changed!" But the Libran Ascendant hasn't really changed at all. He or she has just been finally pushed onto the ropes and is making a long overdue stand.

How might these dynamics be avoided?

If you have Libra rising, *listen* if your partner says, "You'll never tell me what you want, then you get angry when I can't read your mind and I give up and do what I want." Steel yourself and *say what you want.* Try saying what you want *first,* without being prompted. Of course you can add right away, "And what would you like to do? Let's talk about it." Then you're *negotiating*, rather than surrendering by reflex. Unless you work for the U.N. or a dispute settlement center, be careful about settling others' differences *for* them, no matter how often you hear that you're good at it. Adults can work things out on their own.

If you have Libra rising, *listen* if your partner says, "I'm afraid to breathe or sit down in this living room. If you don't want a coffee table I can put my feet on in here, how about having one in the den?" Or if your partner says, "You know, I'd really like to see you with your hair messed up once in a while. You don't have to look perfect all the time. And I'm not sure those high-heeled boots are the best shoes for boulder scrambling."

Finally, if you have Libra rising and you're being bullied and your partner won't negotiate, *stand your ground.* Immediately. Whatever it takes. The situation will only grow worse if you don't.

If you have Libra rising, think about what most influences your choice of partner. Of course you're drawn to Arian fire, drive and directness. In an evolutionary sense, these people are modeling for you how to know what you want and how to go after it, so that your Libran mask won't stay so careful about not rocking the boat that the boat never even leaves the dock. But are you looking *only* for someone to play bad cop to your good cop and fight your battles for you, so that you remain everyone's favorite nice person?

The Vehicle and the Terrain: The first day of Libra is the autumnal equinox, the first day of autumn. The air grows cooler and the days begin to shorten, although light and dark start in balance upon the equinox. The animal kingdom notices these changes and becomes very alert to the environment. A person with Libra rising arrived on the planet with a vehicle—the Libran Ascendant—that's meant to move through life as an ongoing exercise in full awareness of one's surroundings, and in the achievement of harmonious relationships with those surroundings. Life is a constant balancing act. That means aiming for *both inner and outer* balance, moderation and harmony. Libra rising needs to form as peaceful, equitable and harmonious a relationship as possible to everything which is not the self, including other people. But that doesn't mean relating *deeply* to *everything* outside the self. What would be moderate or balanced about that? Sometimes the most peaceful relationship to a person, an artwork or an idea is a distant one, sometimes a close one, sometimes a creative one. The experiential fuel this Libra vehicle needs is anything that can help with the formation of relationships, aesthetic ones and human ones. It's also anything that helps this person stay centered, as if he or she thrives best in something like that balance between the opposites of Day and Night that we see at the equinox. There are many such pairs of opposites. Your needs and mine. Yin and yang. Summer and winter, open and closed . . . Jung called this process "maintaining the tension between the opposites," or "maintaining the awareness of both polarities," and it's the quintessential Libran balancing act. The terrain, then, is anywhere that's navigated by an awareness of opposites: in colors, people, sounds, ideas, etc.

These people do well to appreciate whatever they find beautiful, harmonious, symmetrical and aesthetically appealing, whether by opposite or by complement. (As I once overheard on a cross-continental flight: "Opposites attract, and complements enhance and support.") It might be a painting. It might be a sunset. It might be a building, or a tune, or a shirt. These people do even better, however, to create beauty themselves. Walk through a museum, *and* take a drawing class. Appreciate a fine meal or a well-decorated home, *and* try out a few recipes or repaint the bedroom. People with Libra rising need to involve their behavior (Ascendant) in the creation of balance and harmony.

The Libra rising vehicle isn't meant to be driven all alone. People with this Ascendant need to form relationships, too, in order to teach themselves about maintaining the balance between Self and Other. If they have a primary partner, they still need close friends. Without a primary partner, they need close friends even more. When a scales or a see-saw are motionless, the least change in the environment or the least shifting of weight can tilt the balance one way or the other. Similarly, a well-working Libran relationship is a living, breathing entity, not static or fixed, and it changes as both partners change. Perhaps someone gives a little more here, but is content because it's been agreed that he or she also gets a little more there. What's essential is that a relationship's inevitable compromises continue to feel *fair* to both parties. Fair isn't necessarily completely equal. A man who's six feet ten inches tall and a child who's six years old are served portions of different sizes at dinner, and those portions are fair, although they aren't equal.

Occupational hazards of this Ascendant include a wired, high-strung, out-of-balance nervousness or anxiety that can occur if the Libra rising person has let the balance tip too far in the partner's direction. In such cases, ongoing negotiation and compromise are the best tactics. Another risk is having so many people in the Libran Ascendant's life who all want some of that warm focused attention that the Libra rising person has no time for a life of his or her own. Sometimes this rising sign simply needs to set boundaries, turn down some invitations and hide behind the answering machine for an evening or three.

In a complicated interpersonal conflict, people with Libra rising can see and, to some extent, identify with everyone else's point of view. They can also see all the pros and cons of any decision they must make. Marry this person or that one? Move to another state or stay put? Another hazard for this Ascendant is letting oneself become immobilized with indecision, to the point where the prospective partner moves on, the employer hires someone else, and the window of opportunity closes. In order to get on with their lives, sometimes people with Libra rising need to pick a path and walk down it without looking back.

Staying Comfortable in the Body: People with this Ascendant tend to be very conscious of their physical appearance. If they translate this awareness into thinking of themselves as just one among many of our world's sources of beauty or aesthetic harmony, and they devote a reasonable amount of time, attention and money for their age and body type to being such a source, then more power to them: they'll feel happier and more centered than if they let themselves go. But if they become obsessed with maintaining the stratospheric standards of beauty seen in the high fashion world or Hollywood, then they're in trouble. Those standards are artificial and change from era to era, even decade to decade. They're attainable by only a minuscule fraction of the population within a certain age span, while aided by an army of stylists, and only for the length of the shoot or the catwalk. The more that someone with Libra rising tries to maintain such unrealistic standards of beauty into old age, the more neurotic and the less calm and centered he or she may become. Such people could even begin to hate their bodies. A motto that works well for Libra rising is "Beauty is more than skin deep." It's an attribute of one's spirit and psyche, far more than anything happening with one's body.

Images for a Costume: The archetypal Justice's robes and scales. Beautiful and becoming clothing and/or makeup, not necessarily in the latest style if that style is ugly. A dozen roses and a box of candy, with Cupid's arrow protruding from the body of the giver or the recipient or both. A wedding gown. Elegant and well-cut attire. An artist's smock. A "truce" or "parlez" flag.

Images for the Vehicle: A luxury car with clean symmetrical lines and a perfectly waxed finish: a Bentley; a Cadillac. A car with a "Just Married" sign. A bicycle built for two. A pair of well-matched horses pulling a carriage. A shiny two-seater coupe. Any vehicle that takes two people to operate. A car with controls for both the driver's and the passenger's seats' positions, heating and cooling.

Images for the Terrain: Guy Gavriel Kay's premise for the working of magic in his *Fionavar Tapestry* fantasy trilogy: magic requires both a Mage and a Source who are bonded to one another as partners. A Mage can perform no magic without drawing on his or her Source. A Source is never a Mage, but willingly consents to have his or her energy so used by that particular Mage.

Any terrain that must be crossed in pairs, or perhaps by cooperation among more than two people rather than alone: a tennis doubles match, a bridge game, a three-legged race, etc. Any terrain that requires give-and-take: a see-saw, a tug-of-war.

The Ambassador's Host Country—Venus's House Position:

Venus's house position represents an area of life where someone with Libra rising particularly needs to seek balance, moderation, beauty, and harmonious relationships.

Venus in the first house: These people need a highly refined, aesthetic and affiliative expression of Libra rising, with many experiences that deepen their capacities to form relationships and to appreciate beauty. They do well to cultivate an art form or creative hobby, and harmonious friendships are just as important as a deeper bond. If they overdo the Ascendant, they can be overly focused on pleasing others, and/or overly focused on appearances.

Venus in the second house: With Venus here, in order to have healthy self-esteem, this person needs to develop confidence in his or her ability to relate well to others and to appreciate beauty. Practicing that ability is therefore important. It's helpful to stay centered and to understand the wisdom of moderation in all things. Care should be taken not to pursue beauty or relationships as mere trophies to prop up one's self-esteem.

Venus in the third house: Someone with Libra rising and Venus in the third house does well to learn to communicate elegantly and eloquently. Cultivating an interest in any of the arts, especially the communicative ones, is most helpful to these people. Unless the rest of the chart is armed for bears, they may need to devote some time and practice to becoming more verbally assertive.

Venus in the fourth house: These people benefit from a lovely home with balanced and harmonious proportions. They prefer a pleasant and agreeable home life. However, it's important for them to resolve inevitable domestic conflicts rather than to surrender and buy "peace" at any price. They do well to comprehend the dynamics of their family of origin, particularly the influence of a Venusian parent.

Venus in the fifth house: With Venus here, a Libran Ascendant needs to make time for relating, creativity, and playful unstructured time. Too much isolation and too many responsibilities will start leaching the pleasure from this person's life, leaving him or her tense and melancholy. These people need initial warmth in relating. They do well to be mindful of a tendency to be so attracted to beauty, slickness or style that they overlook more substantial character traits.

Venus in the sixth house: Someone with Libra rising and this Venus placement benefits from meaningful work or mentoring that allows him or her full use of the Venus function: relating, counseling, creating, appreciating beauty, etc. They prefer a working environment characterized by harmony and cooperation, but should take care not to make too many compromises.

Venus in the seventh house: With Venus here, this person benefits from relationships with gentle, gracious, cultivated people. He or she can become more centered and develop more self-understanding through the medium of such intimacy. Libran Ascendants with this Venus placement do well to avoid vain, seductive people, and not to project any unmet needs to feel attractive onto "trophy" partners.

Venus in the eighth house: A Libran Ascendant with this Venus position needs to feel that the bond with a mate involves tremendous mutual sensitivity, rapport and trust. Such a partner can help this person feel safer about venturing into the eighth house's psychologically charged contents: sexuality, death, the occult, and "shadow" material. These people should take care not to value beauty in a mate so highly that nothing else about him or her matters.

Venus in the ninth house: With Venus as this person's guiding star, relating and aesthetics provide life with its greatest meaning. A life without an "I-thou" connection, or a life without beauty, won't feel much worth living. Sometimes these people and their partners should undertake a kind of Venusian "pilgrimage:" perhaps to a museum they've always wanted to see, and/or to some romantic destination such as the Taj Mahal.

Venus in the tenth house: People with Libra rising and this Venus placement do well to have a public identity or avocation using their Venusian energy: counseling; cooperative enterprises; creative professions. They are symbolizing Venus both personally (Libra rising) and professionally (the Ascendant's ruler in the tenth house); so Venusian work helps ground their Libran persona. They should avoid extremely stressful or impersonal jobs.

Venus in the eleventh house: With Venus here, someone with Libra rising will increasingly need associates who promote the continued flourishing of his or her Venus function: "cultural creatives;"

therapists; negotiators; artists; etc. Goals should include becoming more interpersonally and aesthetically aware and skilled with age.
Venus in the twelfth house: People with Libra rising and this Venus placement need inner work on a regular basis, creatively or in partnership or both. Their "inner guru" is Venus, suggesting that all their relationships can potentially help their spiritual growth. Perhaps sometimes a partner inspires them, or perhaps they sometimes trip over their own egotism in a relationship. They should avoid escapist tendencies around pleasures or relating.

ASCENDANT IN SCORPIO:

The Symbols: This person has come into the world wearing the mask of the Psychoanalyst, Hypnotist, Shaman or Detective. Other images for Scorpio rising are the Occultist, Sorcerer, Spy or Hospice Worker. Less than optimal manifestations of this Ascendant might include the Intensity Junkie, the Manipulator, the Brooder or Gollum (from *The Lord of the Rings*).

The Style: This Ascendant is complicated, so we'll spend some extra time here.

Imagine you're on a blind date with someone who knows you're a brilliant, groundbreaking and incredibly skilled and perceptive psychoanalyst, or forensic pathologist, or FBI profiler. How comfortable do you think your date feels? You know that your date knows this about you. How comfortable do *you* feel?

A man or woman with Scorpio rising has reached an evolutionary stage where he or she should present a penetrating, intense and probing face to the world. To minimize the possibility of others' negative reactions to such a mask, the development of a certain level of psychological awareness of oneself and others is essential here.

Basically, someone with Scorpio rising does well to realize that he or she tends to have a powerful unconscious mind. What does that mean? Material from his or her unconscious floats up into this person's awareness more frequently than in people who don't have a lot of Scorpio, Plutonian or eighth house energy in their birth charts, and who can therefore better repress whatever "shadow" material makes them uncomfortable—ambivalent or inappropriate feelings, painful memories, insights about people's Freudian slips and unconscious motives, etc. Although Scorpio Ascendants can have their blind spots, they can be far more perceptive about their own shadow functions than the average person is. Although they are by no means always right, Scorpio Ascendants can often be very perceptive about other people's shadows, too, as if this rising sign came equipped with psychological X-ray vision.

If someone with a Scorpio Ascendant is unaware that not everyone's "vehicle" is also equipped with these in-depth psychological sensors, then he or she can attribute all kinds of motives to another person that simply aren't in that person's conscious thoughts. After a few too many accusations of suspiciousness or of having their minds in the gutter—"How could you say such a thing?!"—Scorpio Ascendants may start keeping their thoughts to themselves. Although developing some discernment and discretion before they speak can be a good thing for these people, emotional isolation never is. Scorpio is a water sign, and water wants emotional connectedness. Scorpio rising benefits from relationships of cathartic and transformative emotional intensity, where they have a partner for their explorations of the psychological underworld. They need their trusted intimates' perspective on their inner landscapes, lest they blow some of their own issues out of proportion.

For Scorpio rising, life should be confronted with honesty, intensity, a commitment to deep self-awareness, and a willingness to examine all taboos. That doesn't mean to break all of them. It just means that no area of life or death should be barred from the laser-sharp scrutiny of this Ascendant.

Taboos are usually assigned to such psychologically charged material as sex, death and the afterlife. This is why kids are told not to discuss religion, the neighbors' divorce, or their uncle's cancer diagnosis at their parents' parties. People with Scorpio rising need some intimates with whom there are no taboo subjects—and they do well not to overuse that X-ray vision with the rest of us.

If the rest of the chart is sensitive and cautious, this Ascendant is intended both to protect this person, and to advertise for the sort of partners who can truly understand him or her. If the rest of the chart is strong and vivid, this Ascendant is intended to express it and to give this person depth and honesty. If the rest of the chart is that of a thinking type or a pragmatic type, this Ascendant is intended to help this person stay in touch with his or her own feelings and with those of other people. All of these types need to be aware that the intensity of their Scorpio masks can seem to convey the desire for a deeper intimacy than they may actually want or should have with everyone whose paths they cross. In such cases, cultivating the ability to use a lighter self-presentation sometimes—more humor, less eye contact, fewer charged topics of conversation, etc.—can be very helpful. In any event, this rising sign's demeanor should transmit the message: "Here is someone who sees deeply into people, who demands frankness and can grasp secrets, and who probably has a few of his or her own."

If the childhood environment was either chaotic, or spent with parents or family members who themselves had powerful unconscious minds and turbulent feelings, then a Scorpio Ascendant with a strong psyche may have felt that he or she had to understand a parent or parents very thoroughly in order to make a deep impact on them. Such an impact may have felt imperative for the Scorpio rising child to achieve, just to capture enough of the parents' attention to get the child's needs met—placating an angry parent, cheering a depressed one, etc. However, Scorpio rising children may also have felt that too *much* notice from a parent or relative might engulf them emotionally or psychologically. In that event, they may have blurted out an occasional home truth in self-defense. They may have been shamed or even punished for verbalizing their perceptions, and may have learned to hide them or even doubt them.

How close was so close that the Scorpio rising child would feel swallowed alive, and how far away was either too far away to get his or her needs met, or too far away to observe and guard against a relative's potentially problematic behavior? Such was the dance that people with Scorpio Ascendants might have needed to learn. Can you imagine how vigilant these people might have therefore had to be, and how much discernment about others they may have had to develop?

In adulthood, this dynamic may translate into wanting to probe into others but not be too deeply probed oneself. Scorpio Ascendants with a less healthy ego structure and a chaotic upbringing may repeat a dynamic of alternately feeling overwhelmed and invaded by intimacy, trying to shut it out completely, or accepting it only if they can control it. But true intimacy works best as a two-way street, so a Scorpio Ascendant may need to choose partners who are more stable than their relatives might have been, and to allow such people to get *and stay* closer than the Scorpio Ascendant may initially find comfortable.

The Persona and the Other—the First House/Seventh House Axis:

People who *overidentify* with a Scorpio Ascendant can display a few different types of behavior.

They may act like an Est facilitator run amok, hammering others with confrontational personal questions that show little or no respect for appropriate boundaries or taboos. ("Why aren't you dealing with your weight problem?" or "How do you feel about your cancer diagnosis?") They may offer cutting psychological observations for which they haven't been asked, which they tend to present as Truth rather than opinion. ("Get real—you'll never reach your potential at work until you've dealt with your father issues.") Particularly if the Scorpio Ascendant is angry, he or she can reduce milder souls to tears with such pronouncements, then criticize them for not being able to handle the Scorpio Ascendant's "honesty."

They may behave like detectives who suspect everyone's motives, and assume everyone is "guilty" until proven innocent. ("The world is full of back-stabbers.") They may do a lot of brooding over the wrongs that others have done them: real or imagined; past, present or anticipated.

They may be so determined to make an impact on others that they behave seductively all the time, or insist that even the most everyday interactions—ordering a meal, getting their teeth cleaned—be fraught with Meaning, Intensity and Memorability. Or, if they've had too many negative responses to such behavior, they may keep their mouths shut but exude a silent, staring intensity that makes everyone in their vicinity uncomfortable.

These examples are of course *not* the typical expressions of healthy Scorpio Ascendants. They are only what may happen with *overidentification* with this Ascendant. (Please see Chapter Two for a discussion of the dynamic of overidentification.)

If these extreme expressions of Scorpio rising occur, how might the seventh-house Other react? It's possible that the Other may be polarized into various extreme Taurean responses.

The Other may cease any attempt at intimate dialogue rather than risk getting napalmed by the Scorpio Ascendant again. Such a decision is rarely announced—Taurus is the least verbal of the signs, and there would be a very high price for such an announcement—but it can be acted on nonetheless. The Other may retreat from the invisible psychological minefield whirling around the Scorpio Ascendant into material or sensory comforts (Taurus) or frivolous, distracting pastimes (Venus rules Taurus), or into the arms of someone who seems to promise calmer waters (Taurus and Venus). "I'll just go get a massage, or go to the mall, or go to the gym, or have lunch with my trainer."

The Other may respond with textbook, set-piece, simplistic "positive thinking" to every dark suspicion raised by the Scorpio Ascendant. "I don't think he's just out to use our daughter. He seems like a nice kid from a stable family. It's normal for teenagers to date. You can't keep her in a cage until she's thirty, you know." The Other may start oversimplifying situations and people as a Taurus-like response to the Scorpio Ascendant's overcomplicating them. "She broke up with you. Stop obsessing and get over it. There are lots of other fish in the sea."

The Scorpio Ascendant may get incensed at the Other's "withdrawal," "shallowness" or "callousness" and respond with a well-aimed psychological stiletto, thereby escalating the conflict. How might this dynamic be avoided?

If you have Scorpio rising, *listen* if your partner says, "Will you please back off and lighten up? Sometimes a cigar is just a cigar!" Or if your partner says, "It's none of your business how their relationship is doing. Don't ask them again." Or if your partner says, "Some people with turbulent or painful lives aren't deep and sensitive and just need some insight. They aren't dealing well with their problems because they *can't,* or they wouldn't have gotten so embroiled in the first place. If you get too close to them, you'll just get dragged down too." Or if your partner says, "Did it occur to you that you could just politely buy a magazine and leave the drugstore? You don't have to snake-charm the clerk. She thought you were hitting on her."

If you have Scorpio rising, think carefully about what most influences your choice of partner. Of course you're drawn to Taurean sensuality and beauty. In an evolutionary sense, your intensity could benefit from that potentially calming and grounded Taurean influence. But you can learn to relax, slow down and remember to take care of your body as well as your psyche without constant prompting. Do you want *only* beauty, and just as a gateway to various soap operatic dramas (such as competition for the Fairest One of All) that will exhaust everyone involved?

The Vehicle and the Terrain: People with Scorpio rising arrived on the planet with a vehicle—their Scorpio Ascendant—that's meant to move through life as an ongoing encounter with the depths of the human psyche, particularly their own. Their unconscious minds have lots of extra entrées to their conscious minds. Therefore, people with this Ascendant need to be willing *to accept everything they feel*. That does *not* mean to act on everything they feel, or even to talk about it. It just means to accept the multiplicity of their feelings, impulses, memories, etc., and to reserve their judgment, if any, for their behavior instead of their emotions. The experiential fuel this Scorpio vehicle needs is an unflinching willingness to face the darkness in ourselves and in our lives. The terrain this vehicle should cover includes the places that carry the most psychological charge and that scare us the most. What are those places? Our damaged, wounded, crazy sides and how they got that way. Our sexuality, not just our physical sexuality, but a consideration of what part of the human being besides the body might form a bond through the sexual act. Our deaths, and a consideration of whatever may lie beyond them.

Scorpio Ascendants can be so skilled at ferreting out others' motivations, wounds, glitches and strong points that they're frequently asked to be others' unofficial or official headshrinkers. That's fine, as long as they don't get so exhausted from being up to their eyebrows in other people's psyches that they neglect the study of their own. It's most helpful to cultivate at least a couple of close friends or intimates with whom the Scorpio Ascendant can be utterly frank about his or her own profound and sometimes unsettling psychological material—like an Ascendant in Libra, the Scorpio vehicle does better with a passenger along for the ride.

This rising sign's occupational hazards include the potential for getting overwhelmed by one's own psyche or that of others, and bogged down in too much brooding. Another hazard can be wading into other people's psyches without getting permission first. Friends who can either listen intently or distract the Scorpio Ascendant for a while are a good antidote. So is learning not to take oneself too seriously all the time. So is learning not to dive so deeply into every human contact that the Scorpio Ascendant winds up with more intimacy than he or she wants or needs.

Staying Comfortable in the Body: More than any other Ascendant, Scorpio rising is aware of its own mortality. It's important not to let that awareness lead to taking stupid risks with one's health—"Everyone's got to die of something"—or to a morbid fear of ageing as a symbol of mortality. It can be helpful to think through one's beliefs about an afterlife. People with this Ascendant can get so absorbed in their psychological lives that they may neglect their bodies. Exercise can be a great way to blow off steam and help put issues into perspective; meeting a good friend for a long walk and a deep conversation might be just the ticket. Understanding their sexuality is particularly important to Scorpio Ascendants. However, a *compulsive or uneasy preoccupation* with sex, to the point where this person thinks of the body only as a sexual instrument, may carry some displacement from a psychological issue that needs processing.

Images for a Costume: A magician's suit and top hat. A scary Halloween costume. A shaman's robes. An undertaker's suit. A psychoanalyst's suit and tie or white coat. A medium's robes; a lens through which one can see ghosts. Darth Vader's black costume and spooky voice and breathing. Hades's cap of invisibility. A vampire's cape. A black leather outfit. A surgeon's mask and gown. The Grim Reaper's robes and scythe.

Images for the Vehicle: Something equipped to fly beneath radar. A Stealth bomber. The Batmobile. A hearse. A broom. A Dodge Viper. A closed black carriage and four black horses. A car with secret weapons. A silent limo with non-see-through, bulletproof glass. Something that can tunnel and excavate beneath the surface. A spaceship with a cloaking device and mind-reading sensors.

Images for the Terrain: The Twilight Zone. The Underworld. A haunted house, literally or metaphorically. A psychoanalyst's office. A hospice or funeral home. A cancer ward. An operating room. A forensic pathology lab or a crime scene investigation. A parapsychology lab. A cemetery. A séance. The Day of the Dead. Terrain that you need psychic powers to cross. Terrain where you must face your deepest fears and your dark side (see the movies *Flatliners* or *Jacob's Ladder,* or think of the boggart in the *Harry Potter* books, which takes the shape of what one most fears).

The Ambassadors' Host Countries—Pluto's and Mars's House Positions:

For a Scorpio Ascendant, one should consider both rulers, Pluto and Mars. Their house positions show where Scorpio rising people can have an extra dose of psychological X-ray vision, where they may be likely to get caught up in their own issues, and therefore where they could most benefit from the courage to face themselves and from some outside perspective.

Pluto or Mars in the first house: This person needs a particularly acute and penetrating expression of Scorpio rising, with lots of experiences that involve self-analysis and exploration of the psychological or even the shamanic underworld (Pluto), or other sorts of extreme fears faced and adventures undertaken (Mars). This potentially edgy persona, if overdone, may be intimidating to others. It may also be depressing to the Scorpio Ascendant if he or she becomes too isolated, so learning to alleviate the Ascendant's impact with humor might be helpful.

Pluto or Mars in the second house: With Pluto here, healthy self-esteem depends on the Scorpio rising person's learning to value his or her intensity and perceptiveness, rather than either exaggerating them or feeling embarrassed by them. With Mars here, self-worth is improved if this person learns to live with courage and pluck, as well as with Scorpionic immediacy. In either case, any tendency toward macho behavior or psychological bullying should be avoided.

Pluto or Mars in the third house: With Pluto here, this person needs to communicate with directness and honesty, but avoid melodrama. Even more information may come from the unconscious mind than is usual with Scorpio rising, so it's not a bad idea to become fluent in dream analysis. (Robert Johnson's book *Inner Work* is a good place to start.) With Mars here, this person's tongue could be a blunt instrument if not wielded with care. Having outlets for intellectual challenge and harmless debate can be a big help.

Pluto or Mars in the fourth house: A Scorpio Ascendant with Pluto here needs to understand how well or poorly the family of origin, particularly one parent, dealt with such Plutonian issues as sexuality, death, and the deep unconscious and its wounds. He or she risks repeating those patterns if they're left unexamined. With Mars here, the focus is on understanding how well or poorly the family, particularly one parent, dealt with anger, assertion, courage, boundaries and drive.

Pluto or Mars in the fifth house: Pluto here indicates a need to create art or humor from one's Plutonian wounds. Art as metaphor, art as therapy, art as releasing and moving on; all are possible. Early in relating, these people should feel that the partner can discuss (not act out!) typically taboo subjects without being scared away. With Mars here, the release of aggression or just plain energy in play or exercise is a great tonic. This person should "fall in like," if not in love, with gutsy, vital people.

Pluto or Mars in the sixth house: With Pluto here, Scorpio rising people need meaningful work and/or mentoring that lets them use their Scorpionic intensity and insight in productive ways. They should beware of so much fascination with the grittier side of life that they accept impossible jobs just to be nose to nose with it. With Mars here, this person needs meaningful work and/or mentoring that feels like an adventure and a challenge. If they don't assert themselves enough on the job, they risk being ground down and burned out.

Pluto or Mars in the seventh house: With Pluto here, this person should accept the inevitable button-pushing presence of the shadow in close relationships—the fact that relating involves jealousy, neediness and projection, not just candy and flowers. Ideally, intimates are psychologically fluent enough to discuss such edgy Plutonian material rather than embody it. With Mars here, the dynamic has more to do with accepting the presence of anger, fear and competition in relating. Both types needs people strong enough to stay in the ring with them.

Pluto or Mars in the eighth house: With Pluto here, ideally, this person's mate needs to find his or her Scorpio Ascendant fascinating and refreshingly honest, rather than invasive or engulfing. Care should be taken that one's mate deals well with his or her own intensity. With Mars here, no cowards need apply for the Scorpio rising's shotgun seat, and anger should be processed quickly lest it fester.

Pluto or Mars in the ninth house: With Pluto here, this person does well with a philosophy of life that involves both facing the grittier truths about oneself and not despairing over the dark side of life. Paradoxically, confronting such matters helps deepen this person's sense that life is worth living. With Mars here, faith in life is heightened by exploring the limits of one's will power and courage.

Pluto or Mars in the tenth house: Pluto here indicates a need for a public identity representing that which Pluto rules: psychological or shamanic depths, honesty, a willingness to look at the dark side of human nature and of one's own psyche. A lower path is to identify with and embody such problematic elements in the psyche. With Mars here, the Scorpio Ascendant needs a public identity as a courageous, frank, even heroic person who takes risks and can handle stress. Both placements need to be careful of burnout.

Pluto or Mars in the eleventh house: With Pluto here, this person needs allies and goals that involve an in-depth exploration of the psyche. In old age, care should be taken not to succumb to the depression that can stem from an unexamined life. With Mars here, a Scorpio rising person needs vital, energetic (though not *too* abrasive) allies and goals, and needs to feel that the future might always hold another adventure . . .

Pluto or Mars in the twelfth house: With Pluto here, a Scorpio Ascendant's "inner guru" counsels a journey to the center of the deep psyche, with the eyes wide open. Extra time spent in this process may yield the calm that can come from heightened self-awareness and a facing of one's own demons. With Mars here, the "inner guru" advises confronting one's fears and living bravely, no matter what. Outward Bound experiences, anyone?

ASCENDANT IN SAGITTARIUS:

The Symbols: This person has come into the world wearing the mask of the Gypsy, the Scholar, the Philosopher, the Anthropologist or the Pilgrim. Other images for Sagittarius include the True Believer, the Professor, the Optimist, the Seeker or the Bon Vivant. Lower level manifestations of this sign's energy might be the Dogmatist, the Proselytizer, the Know-It-All, the Gullible One or the Dissipated One.

The Style: First, a comment about Sagittarius and Gemini may be helpful: they have more in common than any other pair of opposing signs. However, a basic and vital difference is that Gemini represents the axis of *observing and collecting raw data,* whereas its opposite sign, Sagittarius, represents the axis of *collating that data and deriving deductions from it.*

The man or woman with Sagittarius rising has reached an evolutionary stage where he or she must present a hearty, tolerant and robust face to the world. These people should develop the ability to explore and experience the world through studying its various patterns—cultural, legal, scientific, ethical, religious, etc. For Sagittarius rising, life should be confronted with willingness, verve, and a desire to understand and to derive meaning from what one sees and experiences. If the rest of the chart is reflective or inward, this Ascendant is intended both as protective coloration, and as a tool to help this person gather experiences to feed the inner life and make it even richer. If the rest of the chart is strongly airy and analytical, this Ascendant is intended to help these people assign some meaning and perspective to their experiences, so they can start to perceive the whole forest as well as each separate tree. If the rest of the chart is slapdash and extraverted, this Ascendant is intended to help lead this person down multiple roads of experience or even excess, roads that with luck will lead to the proverbial palace of wisdom. In any case, this Ascendant's demeanor should convey the message: "Here is a plucky, expansive, spontaneous and upbeat person who's hungry for experience, who's willing to assign meaning to life and to operate ethically."

If the family of origin had upwardly mobile aspirations, a Jupiter-ruled Sagittarius rising person can be particularly apt to buy into and try to model whatever portion of the bigger-and-better "great American dream" prevailed in that household. Maybe it was the Horatio Alger story. Maybe it was a belief that education is always an all but holy end in itself. Maybe it was get-rich-quick schemes or prosperity consciousness. Maybe it was some form of self-righteous religion or philosophy that bordered on fundamentalism. It can take time for someone with this Ascendant to figure out whether he or she actually shares the family's belief system, and how to avoid being damaged by any of its unrealistic expectations. If the childhood environment included a rolling-stone-gathers-no-moss parent and/or a family system inclined to chaos and to promising more than could be delivered, a stronger person may get suspicious, learn to value stability and reliability as well as flash and bombast, and escape relatively unscathed. A weaker person may spend a long time waiting for various Prize Patrols to deliver their promised fortunes, and be continually let down until he or she learns to be more realistic and recognize pie-in-the-sky offers. All these types need to learn that they and everyone else on the planet are mere mortals prone to inconsistencies and failures.

The Persona and the Other—the First House/Seventh House Axis:

Someone who *overidentifies* with a Sagittarian Ascendant can display a few different types of behavior.

One type is similar to Gemini rising's possible "eternal adolescent" syndrome: a desire to keep all one's options open forever, and a concomitant avoidance of commitments or restrictions of any kind. This man still has no girlfriend, fixed domicile or steady job, because there are still so many girls to meet, places to go and things to do that he just isn't ready to be tied down yet—and this man is eighty-seven years old. Younger and older versions of this type may be inclined to various excesses, all in the name of Experience. There can be a Jupiter-ruled feeling of innate entitlement to whatever is the best, most beautiful, hip, opulent, luxurious, etc. These people may sometimes be loud, brash and exuberant to the point of displaying a rather alarming lack of basic social skills.

Another type of behavior is the eternal professor, the know-it-all, constantly "educating" people who have not asked for his or her information. Another type is the true believer: God or the equivalent is in direct contact with this person, and all the complexity of life is funneled into one rigid belief system into which everything and everyone must fit. If tragedy strikes, it's reacted to solely from this belief system, as if by rote or reflex—"It was God's will" or "It was her karma"—and even grief may be suppressed. Self-righteousness can reign, but all too easily crack and slip into self-indulgence, which is why the flaming moralists of this world are occasionally caught with their pants down . . .

These examples are of course *not* the typical expressions of healthy Sagittarian Ascendants. They are only what can happen with *overidentification* with this Ascendant. (Please see Chapter Two for a discussion of the dynamic of overidentification.)

If these extreme expressions of Sagittarius rising occur, how might the seventh-house Other react? It's possible that the Other may be polarized into various extreme Geminian responses.

The Other may resist any pontifical lectures from Sagittarius rising. "You can't *know* all that stuff you're spouting. You can't prove it. You're not always right. Give me even one fact (Gemini) to support that hairbrained theory (Sagittarius)."

The Other may collude in the Sagittarian Ascendant's endless quest for new experiences, but balk at assigning any lasting or *a priori* meaning to them, or keep computer-like track (Gemini) of the string of broken promises that might accompany them.

The Other may find some manifestations of Sagittarius rising too crude and naïve and boorish for words, and retreat into a posture of intellectual distance. "You're just a jock with no appreciation for Shakespeare or semiotics."

Challenged, the Sagittarian Ascendant can respond with some version of "God's on my side," or with accusations of "effete, pointy-headed intellectualism," which only alienate the Other still further. How might this dynamic be avoided?

If you have Sagittarius rising, *listen* if your partner says, "I'm not sure you have a direct line to God or Truth here. Other points of view might be perfectly valid and not immoral." Or if your partner says, "I need to slow down for a while. I'm not Indiana Jones and I'm not sure you are either." Or if your partner says, "It's okay not to know everything, and not to try to teach it, either." Learn to *agree to disagree.* Learn to find opinions other than yours *interesting,* rather than threatening or "evil" or "just plain wrong."

If you have Sagittarius rising, think carefully about what most influences your choice of partner. Of course you're drawn to Gemini's vivacity, curiosity and openness to new ideas. In an evolutionary sense, you need to learn from Gemini's perceptiveness and lack of prejudice, because those qualities help keep you from being too rigid, dogmatic or even fanatical about your own point of view. But are you looking *only* for someone with whom you can permanently stay in the role of sage or even guru, while they play the wide-eyed ingenue soaking up all your wisdom? Of course you're drawn to Gemini's restlessness and desire for an interesting life. But are you looking *only* for someone to potentiate your own tendency to bite off more experiences than any mortal has time or energy to digest?

The Vehicle and the Terrain: A person with Sagittarius rising has arrived on the planet with a vehicle—the Sagittarian Ascendant—that is meant to move through existence as a wide-ranging, freewheeling scavenger hunt for the meaning of life. What is that meaning? Whatever the Sagittarian Ascendant decides it is, over the course of lots of ongoing research, exploration, experimentation, and informal (or formal) philosophizing. This rising sign needs terrain involving plenty of exposure to new and exotic experiences, and to views of the world that differ from his or her own. The goal is not only to arrive at one's own theories about the meaning of life, but to compare one's theories with those of others. The experiential fuel this Sagittarian vehicle needs can be thought-provoking, inspiring and exciting. It may produce culture shock, or it might call for a response rooted in one's own ethics. The terrain that this vehicle should cover not only allows but encourages the Sagittarius rising person to explore the various patterns and systems—cultural, scientific, religious, etc.—that underlie, permeate or attempt to explain reality.

These people need periodic immersion in an unfamiliar environment, a different mind set or a new and colorful experience. Why? Because such exposure keeps them from getting too rigidly attached to their own world view, and because it's grist for the mill of their own evolving belief system.

Occupational hazards of Sagittarian Ascendants include overextension from their sheer appetite for life in the fast lane—it helps to remember that they too are subject to the limitations of the flesh. Another risk is avoiding all commitments or restrictions, and winding up lonely or with a dearth of either accomplishments or stability. Life *must mean something* to people with this Ascendant, and without Meaning assigned to their existence, they feel crazy and uncentered. But they need to remember that not everyone does or should share their beliefs, or they risk gracelessly trying to shove their theory *du jour* down others' throats.

Staying Comfortable in the Body: People with this Ascendant tend to feel so good when they're out exploring the world that it's usually not hard for them to stay physically active. Problems can arise if someone with Sagittarius rising starts to think she's immortal and doesn't need rest, or if his appetite for the good life leads to too much overindulgence in rich food and other pleasures. That latter dynamic probably has something to do with Jupiter's rulership of both Sagittarius and the liver. Like Gemini rising, Sagittarius rising people do well to recall that the healthier their bodies are, the less restricted their lives will be, and the more interesting experiences they can gather.

Images for a Costume: An Indiana Jones hat and travel gear. A gypsy's costume. A cowboy's garb. A pilgrim's robes. A professor's cap and gown. A British lawyer's robes and wig. The gown and banquet table of the Ghost of Christmas Present (from *A Christmas Carol*). A Santa suit. An outfit one would wear on safari. Offshore sailing gear.

Images for the Vehicle: Something fully-equipped for long-distance travel through any kind of territory. A hydroplane. A helicopter. A gypsy caravan. A maximum horse-powered Range Rover. Something one would drive on safari. A deep space exploration vehicle. An ocean-worthy ship; the "tall ships" and colonizing vessels of the past. A cross-country train. A jet equipped and powered to fly long distances.

Images for the Terrain: A trip to any foreign country or region. A world tour, with the proviso that anywhere this person stopped, he or she had to learn something new and make a new friend. A pass to any university classes that interest this person. An anthropology expedition. A street with churches, temples and mosques from every religion in the world. An international bazaar. The United Nations. Babylon Five (a space station city where dozens of cultures try to coexist). Anywhere this person would experience culture shock.

The Ambassador's Host Country—Jupiter's House Position:
   Jupiter's house position is where someone with Sagittarius rising most needs to face the world with optimism and expansiveness, and attempt to live according to his or her ideals.
Jupiter in the first house: This person needs a particularly robust expression of Sagittarius rising, full of tolerance, humor and exuberance. A double dose of horizon-broadening experiences that expose these people to different mindsets would be helpful. Life is a kaleidoscope here, and this person needs to discover as many of its patterns as possible. If the Ascendant is overdone, these people can be convinced they've found the One and Only Truth, or feel entitled

to all kinds of excesses, as if they were "King of the Gods" rather than flesh and blood.

Jupiter in the second house: With Jupiter here, in order to have healthy self-esteem, this person needs to develop an expansive, optimistic attitude and a willingness to try new activities. Evolving one's own ethical system is helpful too. So is feeling that life holds possibilities rather than closed doors. Care should be taken not to equate one's self-worth with luxury items or various status symbols whose common denominator is their snob appeal.

Jupiter in the third house: Men and women with Sagittarius rising and Jupiter in the third house will find that communicating in any form lifts their spirits and heightens their sense that life is worth living. They need to communicate colorfully and inspiringly, and humor is always a plus. They also need to avoid bombast, preaching and hyperbole, and to remember that objectivity may not be their innate strong suit.

Jupiter in the fourth house: A Sagittarian Ascendant with Jupiter here does well to create a home that feels like a tonic. Such a nest needn't interfere with how much this Ascendant typically relishes and benefits from travel. A home that lifts the mood creates a nourishing base to support the gathering of new experiences. These people do well to understand the influence of a Jupiter-like parent, and not let themselves be overshadowed by him or her.

Jupiter in the fifth house: These people need a periodic dose of Jupiter-ruled activities to maintain their fifth house *joie de vivre*: travel, new ideas, exotic people and locales, inspired silliness, or creativity that involves over-the-top performance and applause. Early in a relationship, the Sagittarian Ascendant with Jupiter in the fifth house should look for positive, optimistic, encouraging people; tortured *artistes* need not apply.

Jupiter in the sixth house: With Jupiter here, someone with Sagittarius rising needs meaningful work and/or mentoring that involves the possibility of positive outcomes—no glass ceilings, no hopelessly stuck clients. These people are natural cheerleaders, able to help their protegés believe in themselves as they never have before. Their work should not contradict their basic ethics. Care should be taken not to shoulder impossible workloads or deadlines no mere mortal could meet.

Jupiter in the seventh house: Intimacy is vital to these people, intimacy with upbeat, hopeful partners with a larger-than-life quality who can guide and inspire the Sagittarian Ascendant, but not get caught up in mutual preaching wars with him or her. Care should be taken neither to project inflated expectations on these partners, nor to become the recipient of such projections.

Jupiter in the eighth house: A Sagittarian Ascendant with this Jupiter placement needs to feel that the mate is an optimistic, resilient and upbeat person—no one making a permanent religion out of gloom and angst need apply. Someone with whom there's a shared belief system is a plus, but at a minimum there should be mutual respect for each other's views. Care should be taken to avoid people with inflated and grandiose notions.

Jupiter in the ninth house: With Jupiter here, a philosophy of life that works for these people has much in common with the power of hope, faith and optimism. Their guiding star is Jupiter, and the ability to see positive outcomes and to work toward win-win situations will help life feel maximally worth living to them. Pettiness, "thinking small," and acting against their ethics should be avoided.

Jupiter in the tenth house: Sagittarian Ascendants with this Jupiter placement do well to have a vocation or avocation that employs their Jupiter functions. Work for benevolent organizations is one possibility, or work that involves guiding, inspiring, coaching, or conveying a positive larger picture to others. So is work involving travel or foreign cultures. The job should not feel either rote, or as if all its possibilities are exhausted and there's no room for growth.

Jupiter in the eleventh house: With Jupiter here, a Sagittarian Ascendant needs associates who help his or her Jupiter function flourish: tolerant, expansive, forward-thinking people who enjoy traveling, philosophizing, and thinking in ways they have not been taught to think. With age, he or she also needs to have *more* faith in life and in positive outcomes, not less. Living according to his or her principles and ideals will become increasingly important.

Jupiter in the twelfth house: Someone with Sagittarius rising and this placement has a Jupiterian "inner guru." This guru would counsel cultivating an attitude of optimism, warmth, inclusiveness, generosity, and finding the good in all people and all situations. Faith, and acting on faith, are important here. As a church's bumper sticker says, "To believe is to care, to care is to do."

ASCENDANT IN CAPRICORN:

The Symbols: This person has come into the world wearing the mask of the Wise Elder, the Prime Minister, the Executive or the Authority. Other images for Capricorn rising include the Strategist, the Hermit, the Realist, or the Architect. Less than optimal manifestations of this Ascendant might include Scrooge, Machiavelli, Atlas Carrying the Weight of the World on His Shoulders, or the Pessimist.

The Style: This man or woman has reached an evolutionary stage where he or she should present a dignified, practical and rather reserved face to the world. Remember that the first day of Capricorn is the first day of winter. Metaphorically, this Ascendant needs to prepare for a "wintry" environment. The development of enough grounded reality-testing, pragmatism and perseverance to achieve personally meaningful accomplishments—"Great Works"—is essential. Life should be confronted with forethought, planning, efficiency, wise use of resources and tremendous self-control. The fuel is any important goal the Capricorn Ascendant has in his her sights, and the terrain is wherever he or she must go in order to achieve that goal.

If the rest of the chart is tempestuous or impulsive, the Capricorn Ascendant is intended to help this person develop enough foresight to think before he or she speaks or acts. If the rest of the chart is gentle and labile, the Capricorn Ascendant is intended to provide enough self-containment and reality-testing to help protect this person's soft underbelly. If the rest of the chart is independent or driven, the Capricorn Ascendant is intended to help this person size up the obstacles to his or her goals and maneuver around them, alone if necessary. In any case, this rising sign's demeanor should convey the message: "Here is a reserved, pragmatic, sensible person who doesn't miss a thing, who can be extremely competent and efficient, who's worthy of respect."

For this wintry Ascendant, anything that feels out of control can feel potentially dangerous—we can freeze to death in the winter unless we control our preparations for a dangerous environment. Childhood is probably the epoch of our lives over which we have the least control, simply by virtue of being children. If the childhood environment was emotionally cold, and love or approval or even acceptance was conditional, a Capricorn Ascendant may have decided to quit trying to get emotional support from a family that couldn't or wouldn't give it. In adulthood, unless this dynamic is examined, these people may give up far too easily on asking for love and connectedness. Meanwhile, they can remain models of whatever overachieving behavior—something they *can* control—that they unconsciously hope will solicit the desired response from their loved ones. If the childhood environment was harsh materially, these people may have decided that their longed-for Security is a pearl beyond price and remain so cautious about any sort of risk—not all of which they can control—that they limit their possibilities in life. If the childhood environment was chaotic, these people may decide to try to control anything or everything that they can possibly control, or they may retreat into distance and negativity. All of these types do well to remember that, as I learned in a counseling skills class, *control is what we try to get when we fear we don't have power.* If controlling behavior appears in the adult lives of people with Capricorn rising, its source may of course be extremely complex. Nevertheless, it might be helpful for these people to ask themselves, "What am I afraid will happen if I don't have control? Where am I afraid I have no power? And did I ever feel anything like this when I was a child?"

The Persona and the Other—the First House/Seventh House Axis:

Someone who *overidentifies* with a Capricorn Ascendant can display a few different types of behavior.

As you've probably gathered from the preceding section, he or she may act like a control freak. He or she may categorically *demand* punctuality or *forbid* certain kinds of food or *insist* that you vote for the same candidates. Such a Capricorn Ascendant can issue edicts on what to wear, how to care for your health, when to send thank-you notes, how to handle your own creative process—the list can seem endless.

Another behavior involves making a near-religion out of what psychologists call compensatory striving. These Capricorn rising people don't feel right about themselves, and they try to compensate by equating their self-worth with what they've accomplished. Woe betide anyone who gets in the way of this Capricorn Ascendant's attempts to get into Harvard law school, become a brain surgeon or win a Pulitzer prize for the Great American Novel.

Another behavior can turn this winter-ruled Ascendant into a security-conscious Ice King or Queen. No real feelings are ever shown—that would be an emotional risk. None of what this Ascendant would call "mad money" is ever spent—that would be a financial risk. No false moves are ever made; everything is planned ahead. Spontaneity is throttled to death.

These examples are of course *not* the typical expressions of healthy Capricorn Ascendants. They are only what can happen with *overidentification* with this Ascendant. (Please see Chapter Two for a discussion of the dynamic of overidentification.)

If these extreme expressions of Capricorn rising occur, how might the seventh-house Other react? It's possible that the Other may be polarized into various extreme Cancerian responses.

If faced with too many breathing lessons from the Capricorn Ascendant, the Other may protest or withdraw, become evasive and secretive, and continue the disapproved behavior behind a Cancerian shell. If faced with compensatory striving, the Other may try to talk the Capricorn Ascendant out of it for a while. "Look at how you're neglecting your health/your relationship/your children!" Or the Other may decide that since the Capricorn Ascendant is overfunctioning in the responsibility department, the Other can do something resembling a Cancerian regression and expect to be taken care of like a child. If faced with cool unavailability, the Other may become twice as emotional in trying to get a rise out of the Capricorn Ascendant—or give up and find warmer harbors.

The Capricorn Ascendant can code all of this behavior as irresponsible and unrealistic, and feel burdened and martyred. He or she can then retreat into still more striving, distance and attempts at control. How might this dynamic be avoided?

If you have Capricorn rising, *listen* if your partner says, "You know, I managed to become an adult without your constant guidance, and I can live through today without it, too." Smile, back off, and figure out what you may be nervous about and are therefore trying to control.

Listen if your partner says, "On your deathbed you won't lie there thinking, "I sure am glad I put in all those 90 hour weeks at the office." Accomplishments *are* important to you, but there's more to living well than your outer-world achievements.

Listen if your partner says, "Don't you have a heart? How do you think I felt when you did that?" Remember what a wise person once said: "People will forget the details of what you did and said and how smart you were, but they will never forget how you made them feel."

If you have Capricorn rising, think carefully about what most influences your choice of partner. Of course you're drawn to Cancerian nurturing qualities. In an evolutionary sense, you can learn from such a person how to soften your own stance in the world, which can be too hard or withdrawn for your own good. But are you looking *only* for a support person who can take care of logistical and domestic details for you? Of course you're drawn to Cancerian empathy and tenderness. But are you looking *only* for someone to deal with others' messy and demanding feelings, or even to carry your own emotions for you so you don't have to feel them? Of course you find Cancerian gentleness appealing. But are you looking *only* for someone who makes you look more responsible and accomplished by contrast, or for someone to "fix" so that you're distracted from your own inner life, and so that you won't risk closeness to a true equal?

The Vehicle and the Terrain: Someone with Capricorn rising has come into the world with a vehicle—the Capricorn Ascendant—that is meant to move through life as an ongoing lesson in how to manifest something from one's inner processes in the physical, material plane. This process is less about creativity in the sense that we normally use that word, and more about bringing something of one's spirit into three-dimensional, time-bound *reality*, so that a record of one's interior life is left in the everyday outer world of form.

This process also requires people with Capricorn rising to toughen up, to become much stronger, more practical and more competent at the end of their lives than they were at the beginning. Why? Because they are learning to develop their innate resources of pragmatism, self-sufficiency, shrewdness and reserve in order to use them to manifest those meaningful accomplishments.

This Ascendant is meant to learn how society works and how to fit into it—how to "win friends and influence people"—in order to use such social awareness and savvy to help the Capricorn rising person attain his or her own goals. Fitting into society should not be an end in itself, but a means to whatever end is truly important for the Capricorn Ascendant. The sign of the Goat, Capricorn needs to climb mountains—the trick is to pick the right ones.

What are some useful strategies for this Ascendant? Self-knowledge is vital here. Time spent alone can help, because it helps develop sufficient inner solitude and self-awareness that the Capricorn Ascendant can learn to distinguish which mountains are most personally relevant from which ones are merely impressive. Self-control, usually abundant with this rising sign, helps the Capricorn rising person stay on track to accomplish its goals. Reserve can be important, too: as the proverb says, "sometimes the pot boils better with the lid on." For this rising sign, absolute integrity is both a higher goal and a strategy to attain that goal. Saying what one means. Meaning what one says. Walking one's talk, so that this Ascendant's *behavior* stays impeccably in line with his or her *intentions*, regardless of his or her fluctuating moods.

The experiential fuel needed by people with this rising sign is *whatever impels them toward and equips them for genuinely meaningful accomplishments*. The terrain is any landscape, no matter how harsh, forbidding or lonely, that they must successfully navigate in order to attain those goals.

Occupational hazards of this rising sign include a kind of frozen, rigid, affectless demeanor that can isolate these people emotionally. Another risk is burnout from overwork or lack of rest. Another hazard is attempting to control the uncontrollable or the behavior of others, which can add to exhaustion and to loneliness as others flee the autocratic Capricorn Ascendant. Another risk can be putting arduous effort into climbing the wrong mountain—here's the person who quits the medical profession at midlife because he or she never really wanted to be a doctor in the first place.

Staying Comfortable in the Body: The body is not a machine, but people with Capricorn rising can sometimes lose sight of that fact and push themselves mercilessly, even sacrificing their health to the attainment of their goals. If they've taken the route of suppressing too many of their emotions (and therefore probably not having particularly meaningful goals or deep intimacy), and of being extremely cautious and generally saying "No" to life, then they may use food for comfort or sleep for escape. It might help them take better care of themselves if they can think of their health as a tool that they need to keep in good working condition for optimal productivity. Staying flexible, both physically and metaphorically, is a good goal here. Yoga, swimming, other exercise that doesn't tighten or restrict the body, and getting some deep tissue massage might all be helpful.

Images for a Costume: A three-piece suit. Pearl studs and low-heeled pumps, or unobtrusive cufflinks and wingtips. Something that "old money" would wear. Conservative, classic, well-tailored clothing constructed to last, but not to call too much attention to oneself. An Elder's robes. A hermit's garb. A miser's bargain clothing. A Swiss Army knife with every possible attachment. A watch with alarms and reminders. A pager, preferably one with an option to buzz oneself, in order to finesse the Capricorn Ascendant out of meetings that take too much time.

Images for the Vehicle: A grey Saab with an onboard GPS. A Volvo with the best crash-test rating available. A seaplane that's also roadworthy. A car or minivan whose trunk, depending on its location, carries: a spare tire, tire iron and jack; jumper cables; up-to-date maps; Fix-A-Flat; a flashlight; a tool kit; kitty litter; a shovel; rock salt; blankets; parkas; rope; water; walkie-talkies; MREs and flares. Any vehicle well-suited and equipped for whatever territory it will cross: no urban SUVs; no dune buggies in Manhattan; no rickshaws in Fairbanks.

Images for the Terrain: A wintry landscape. A mountain slope. Territory where progress is measured in increments. A demanding graduate program with proficiency tests looming ahead. Territory where one has to make the proper preparations and expend great effort in order to navigate or even survive. A harsh, unforgiving environment: Antarctica, a tiny space station, etc. Territory where you have to keep a cool head and not give in to your feelings. Territory where you have to travel at least part of the journey alone.

The Ambassador's Host Country—Saturn's House Position:
An important clue to the nature of this Ascendant's centering "Great Work" can lie in Saturn's house position. Also, here is where the Capricorn rising person most needs to relate to the world as if it were winter: with practicality and forethought, but without rigidity or frozen feelings.

Saturn in the first house: This person needs a particularly grounded expression of Capricorn rising, with lots of experiences that involve meaningful accomplishments—Great Works—achieved with integrity and self-discipline. Developing a certain amount of reserve and self-sufficiency is important. If this person overdoes the Ascendant, he or she could become overly controlled and controlling and therefore emotionally isolated, or perhaps pursue the wrong goals for reasons related to status or survival.

Saturn in the second house: For healthy self-esteem, these people need to feel competent to accomplish Great Works alone if necessary, performing marvels of efficiency, organization and reality-testing. Care should be taken not to shoulder too many personally meaningless responsibilities just to prove that this person can suffer alone. These people should also avoid a bootstrap mentality that refuses to get financial help or even information to help meet their goals, when student loans, for example, may be quite possible and needn't mean lifelong indebtedness.

Saturn in the third house: Someone with Capricorn rising and Saturn in the third house does well to develop Saturnian perception skills: logical, rigorous, thorough and utterly grounded in reality. He or she may be drawn to a Great Work that involves mastering and/or communicating about a structured body of knowledge. Care should be taken to discuss one's feelings when and as necessary.

Saturn in the fourth house: These people benefit from an organized, orderly and well-functioning home, which can feel like their austere and clean-lined "tower room," but shouldn't be overly Spartan. It's helpful to analyze their family of origin for how love might have been conditional, what those conditions were, and how a patriarchal or cold parent might have influenced this person.

Saturn in the fifth house: With Saturn here, a Capricorn Ascendant needs pleasures, hobbies and "down time" that involve his or her Saturn function: self-discipline, organization and structure. A hobby or art that one has to practice in order to master is a good possibility, as is building something that takes time and patience. Early in relationships, this person needs demonstrations of integrity from the partner, and a certain amount of reserve.

Saturn in the sixth house: Someone with Capricorn rising and this Saturn placement does well to have meaningful work that allows him or her to use Saturnian skills: management ability; efficiency; pragmatism; and the willingness to work alone if necessary. Care should be taken not to assume more than one's share of responsibility. Mentors and protégés should be wise, realistic, self-disciplined and productive people.

Saturn in the seventh house: With Saturn here, this person benefits from relationships with reliable, grounded, mature people. Ideally, such partners are self-actualized and have tremendous integrity, and are not repressive, fearful or withholding. If the Capricorn Ascendant feels truly respected by his or her intimates, and does not demand that the partner carry the Saturn function for both parties, those are good signs.

Saturn in the eighth house: A Capricorn Ascendant with this Saturn placement needs to feel that the bond with a mate involves mutual respect, an honoring of one another's autonomy and accomplishments, and a resolve to treat one another with absolute integrity. Relationships operating on a lesser level will lose their appeal. Care should be taken not to shut down and give up entirely on relating when these conditions aren't met.

Saturn in the ninth house: With Saturn here, developing healthy self-sufficiency and the persistence to achieve satisfying accomplishments will help make this person's life more meaningful. Evolving a philosophy of life that involves integrity and self-reliance, rather than isolation, negativity or a "bunker mentality," would also be beneficial.

Saturn in the tenth house: These people need to fill the shoes of the Wise Elder, both in terms of their self-presentation (Capricorn Ascendant) and their public identity (tenth house Saturn). Sometimes it takes years and a great deal of determination and solitary effort before they can assume such a mantle. Without the right vocation, they can risk feeling grimly resigned to a restrictive and drab job.

Saturn in the eleventh house: With Saturn here, the Capricorn Ascendant needs associates who encourage the ongoing development of his or her Saturn qualities: realism; integrity; efficiency, etc. This person's goals should allow for the increasing importance of meaningful achievements and self-sufficiency—not loneliness—as he or she ages.

Saturn in the twelfth house: Someone with Capricorn rising and this placement of Saturn needs some time spent on inner work on a regular basis. His or her guru is the proverbial Wise Elder, who would counsel a rigorous, disciplined, committed approach to spiritual matters: Tai Chi; yoga; a focused meditative practice with measurable steps.

ASCENDANT IN AQUARIUS:

The Symbols: This person has come into the world wearing the mask of the Individualist, Rebel, Genius or Truth-Sayer. Other images include the Non-Conformist, Mutant, Inventor, Alien or Geek. Less than optimal expressions of this Ascendant's energy might include the Weirdo, Sociopath, Crackpot or Flake.

The Style: In some ways, this is the hardest Ascendant to describe, because someone responding really well to Aquarius rising expresses it in such an utterly unique way that it's hard to foresee or predict.

This man or woman has reached an evolutionary stage where he or she should present an original, unconventional and highly individual face to the world. Development of the abilities to question authority and not automatically follow the crowd is essential. Life should be confronted with as much independence as possible, independence of mind, heart, will and spirit. People wearing the mask of the Rebel need to make sure they're fighting the War of Aquarian Independence in the right place. If a symbolic battleground is chosen instead—such as the office dress code—Aquarian Ascendants can simply look difficult, contrary and "different." Meanwhile they're avoiding the real issue, which is that they've succumbed to parental pressures to choose a job that doesn't suit them and never will.

If the rest of the chart is relationship-oriented and empathic, the Aquarian Ascendant is intended to keep this person from dissolving into the partner, family or friends. If the rest of the chart is lively and playful, the Aquarian Ascendant is intended to help this person express his or her unique vision. If the rest of the chart is strong and driven, the Aquarian Ascendant is intended to help reinforce this person's pursuit of his or her own goals. In any case, this Ascendant should convey the message: "Here is someone who's not cut from the same cloth as anyone else on this planet, who is very much his or her own person, who follows the proverbial different drummer."

If the childhood environment was unpredictable, particularly if one or both parents chafed, even unconsciously, at the responsibilities of parenting, people with this Ascendant may have reacted a few different ways. They may have detached from the family emotionally or otherwise, either because they didn't get good enough modeling from that family about how to be close, or because they expected the other shoe to drop and their ambivalent parents to disappear at any moment, or both. If the family was particularly chaotic or dysfunctional, this Air sign Ascendant can carry a "wired," high-strung, vigilant energy, as if expecting a nasty surprise at any moment. Even with a good childhood, the match between the temperament of the Aquarian Ascendant and that of the rest of the family is often poor, and the Aquarius rising person can feel as if his or her parents might have taken the wrong baby home from the hospital. In any case, even if it was safe to belong to that family, something about Aquarius rising people didn't fit into their childhood environment. They do well to learn that "being different" doesn't necessarily mean being lesser or worse, that they don't have to feel like the outcast or the misfit everywhere in their adult lives, and to value their uniqueness.

The Persona and the Other—the First House/Seventh House Axis:

People who *overidentify* with an Aquarian Ascendant can display a few different types of behavior. If they're fighting a symbolic and displaced War of Aquarian Independence, they may go in for gratuitous weirdness that doesn't help them individuate. "I insist on *always* eating dessert first, even at a five-hundred-dollar-a-plate fundraiser." They'll be contrary by reflex. "You say black, I say white. You say goodbye, and I say hello." They stubbornly won't compromise over even the smallest details, as if giving in feels like something akin to dying. However, this type is at least still actively battling for individuality, albeit in the wrong place. Another type has temporarily surrendered; such a person is detached and unavailable. They may say all the right things, but they're not fully engaged in the conversation. That typically clear Aquarian gaze can turn cold and remote as they retreat into themselves more deeply—overidentifying with this Ascendant may spell a lonely path through life. Finally, because this sign represents the tension between Self and Society, someone who's overidentified with an Aquarian Ascendant can become more and more isolated from society and disdainful of even its life-affirming and necessary laws. At the very end of this antisocial path can lie not just isolation but sociopathy.

These examples are of course *not* the typical expressions of healthy Aquarian Ascendants. They are only what may happen with *overidentification* with this Ascendant. (Please see Chapter Two for a discussion of the dynamic of overidentification.)

If these extreme expressions of Aquarius rising occur, how might the seventh-house Other react? It's possible that the Other may be polarized into various extreme Leonine responses.

If the Aquarian Ascendant is overly distant, the Other may start various acting-out, attention-getting behaviors, which may become more flamboyant (Leo the Performer) if the Other continues to get an unsatisfactory response. If the Aquarian Ascendant is extremely contrary, the Other may try to impose his or her will autocratically (Leo the Sovereign). If the Aquarian Ascendant is engaged in a highly eccentric form of symbolic rebellion, the Other may try to get him or her to be more pleasing to others and stop making waves (stop embarrassing the Leonine "royal family"). People overidentifying with an Aquarian Ascendant can react badly to any hint of being told what to do or of being controlled in any way, as if that were a terrible invasion of their boundaries. They may well respond by redoubling whatever behavior set off the Other in the first place.

How might this dynamic be avoided?

If you have Aquarius rising, *listen* if your partner says, "Hello! Is anybody home? Pay *attention* to me! Pay attention to *me!*" You might want to ask yourself what declaration of independence you're avoiding by that detached behavior. If you're "not really there," think carefully about where you'd rather be instead.

If you have Aquarius rising, *listen* if your partner throws up his or her hands in exasperation and says "Just do it." You don't have to comply, but you'd do well to figure out why you're being so resistant—what part of your individuality you may feel is at stake.

If you have Aquarius rising, *listen* if your partner says, "Would it kill you to do something normal for a change?" (Attend the office Christmas party, heat the house in the winter, close the shower curtain, etc.) This point is delicate, if you have Aquarius rising; you are not supposed to behave just like everyone else. But it's a better use of your energy to defend the freedoms that most matter to you, *that are about your essence,* and not to waste your energy squabbling over what's ultimately inconsequential.

If you have Aquarius rising, think carefully about what most influences your choice of partner. Of course you're drawn to Leo's warmth, radiance and air of self-assurance. In an evolutionary sense, you can learn a lot from someone who's comfortable and happy in his or her own skin, and for whom attention doesn't provoke the fear of being ostracized. But are you *only* projecting your own need to form a healthy individuated ego onto someone who appears to have such a strong one? Of course you're drawn to Leo's natural authority—but does it *only* symbolize some authority you've not claimed over your own life? Finally, have you picked an authoritarian person only so you can distract yourself by being in constant symbolic rebellion against him or her, rather than putting all that Aquarian energy toward figuring out who you yourself are?

The Vehicle and the Terrain: A person with Aquarius rising has arrived on the planet with a vehicle—the Aquarian Ascendant—that is meant to move through life as an ongoing exercise in learning how to think for oneself. How many meals a day should we eat? How much time alone do we need? Other than their anatomy, what are the differences between men and women? When an Aquarian Ascendant considers those questions and a million others, he or she needs to get past the need for social approval and the instinct to conform. Whether they're living in Berkeley in 1968, Washington D.C. in 1861, London in 1776 or your hometown today, people with Aquarius rising should resist being overly influenced by the opinions of the day.

The goal isn't a blind resistance of all tradition and authority—that's being just as influenced by authority as someone who always surrenders to it. Rather, the strategy is to *question* authority, to *question* the status quo, in order to achieve the goal of figuring out for oneself how one wants to live. The experiential fuel that people with this rising sign need is whatever most pushes them to be themselves—sometimes that fuel will be a supportive friend, sometimes a petty tyrant. The terrain is anywhere one has to think for oneself in order to navigate.

Occupational hazards of this rising sign include having such a knee-jerk adversarial response to *any* kind of authority or received wisdom that this person narrows his or her opportunities in life by flunking out of school, winding up in jail, having a baby out of wedlock at age 15, etc. Another risk for people with this rising sign can be feeling like such an outsider that they may eventually quit trying to connect with others. As a social species, human beings need *some* friendly contact with one another; cooperation is partly why we've killed mastodons, planted wheat, survived and evolved. If individuality becomes permanent isolation, we're in trouble—that's why solitary confinement is considered a punishment. Another hazard can be so much egregious symbolic rebellion or so much distancing behavior that others are permanently alienated.

Staying Comfortable in the Body: Aquarius tends to be more comfortable in the realm of ideas than in the body. In the mythology of Aquarius's ruling planet, the god Uranus devoured his own children because they weren't physically perfect. This rising sign may not be in pursuit of a physical aesthetic ideal. Rather, the body can be experienced as *inconvenient*: it has instincts and needs that, from the Aquarian point of view, may threaten to control this person. An über-first-house-Aquarian friend told me one day, "It took me a long time to realize that my body is an animal that I live in, and I have to feed it right and let it get enough sleep or it will interfere with all the stuff I want to do." If you have Aquarius rising, take that message to heart: a reasonably strong, healthy and well-rested body can and will help you walk the path of individuation.

Images for a Costume: Clothes and a haircut that signal rebellion for whatever era, culture or subculture in which the Aquarius rising person lives, or that just don't fit into that person's society and culture. Summer-of-love hippie garb on Wall Street. A beatnik's turtleneck sweater and beret in an operating room. Punk or grunge clothing at the opera. Anything completely original. Anything the Bionic Man or Woman would wear. Anything made only for that person's body.

Images for the Vehicle: The most cutting-edge spaceship imaginable. A time machine. The Green Goblin's flying surfboard (in the *Spiderman* series). James Bond's gadget-loaded car. The Air Force's latest model jet. A car covered with decorations, or that otherwise doesn't resemble any other car on earth—one in my town is completely plastered with all kinds of dolls, like a new kind of folk art. A car whose door is unlocked only by the owner's thumbprint or retinal scan.

Images for the Terrain: The Outer Limits. Anywhere the "rules" don't work. An anarchy. A technocracy. Utopia. Anywhere a revolution is in progress. Terrain *where you must think for yourself* in order to navigate. If this is a fairy tale, a place where no one else's maps will work for you, and yours will work only if you explored the place and drew the maps for yourself. If this is science fiction, a place where the laws of the physics you know do not apply, or a place where you are an alien being in a foreign culture, and it shows.

The Ambassadors' Host Countries—Uranus's and Saturn's House Positions:

For Aquarius rising, both of its rulers, Uranus and Saturn, should be considered. Their house positions can show where the Aquarian Ascendant most needs to develop true individuality and independence, rather than act out an empty symbolic rebellion.

Uranus or Saturn in the first house: This person needs a particularly striking expression of Aquarius rising, with lots of experiences that involve personal choice and the claiming of one's own unique path through life. With Uranus here, the development of independence and the willingness to act on one's individuality are essential. With Saturn here, integrity and a resolve not to alter one's behavior just to win approval are both emphasized. If this person overdoes the Ascendant, he or she could move so far in the direction of the self and away from society that social ostracism or even sociopathy might become risks.

Uranus or Saturn in the second house: For healthy self-esteem with Uranus here, these people need to get past caring about others' opinions of them. The more they're being themselves, the better they'll feel *about* themselves. With Saturn here, these people need to feel self-reliant and competent in order to maintain a sense of self-worth. Both types need to avoid behavior that would be inauthentic *for them*, just for the sake of financial security.

Uranus or Saturn in the third house: Someone with Aquarius rising and Uranus in the third house does well to develop Uranian perception skills: questioning clichés and received ideas, thinking and communicating independently, and avoiding censorship. With Saturn here, this person does well to cultivate a practical turn of mind and the ability to communicate logically and clearly. Both types may need encouragement to discuss their feelings as much as they should.

Uranus or Saturn in the fourth house: With Uranus here, these people do well to apply their individuality to their home environment. Who says they can't turn the living room into a bedroom and the master bedroom into an office? With Saturn here, privacy becomes particularly important. Both types do well to consider whether their families of origin were either unstable or overly controlling and cold, and whether they overadapted to that early environment.

Uranus or Saturn in the fifth house: With Uranus here, this person needs pleasures and unstructured time that relate to his or her Uranian function: unusual, non-mainstream, offbeat hobbies without a paint-by-numbers approach. Early in relationships, they appreciate a refreshingly original person. With Saturn here, creative outlets can require more focus and practice, and first dates will go better if they're with responsible, organized people.

Uranus or Saturn in the sixth house: With Uranus here, an Aquarius rising person benefits from meaningful work where he or she can be as original and innovative as possible. Self-employment would be a huge plus. With Saturn here, the work can involve more organization, focus and solo effort, and care should be taken not to assume more than one's share of responsibility. Both types need to make very sure they can be themselves on the job as much as possible.

Uranus or Saturn in the seventh house: With Uranus here, these people do well to cultivate relationships with people who encourage them to be themselves, or who even demand it. Ideally, such partners are also highly individuated. With Saturn here, partners should demonstrate their realism and reliability, and there should be tremendous mutual respect. Both types need to avoid clinging vines, and to avoid projecting onto their partners either their own independence (Uranus) or their own capacity for responsibility (Saturn).

Uranus or Saturn in the eighth house: An Aquarian Ascendant with Uranus here needs to feel that the bond with the mate involves a bedrock appreciation of his or her autonomy and uniqueness. These people should be willing to break the "rules" about mate selection—the best partner for them may be the last person Mom and Dad would have picked. With Saturn here, these people need integrity and commitment from the mate. Both types need to avoid withdrawing emotionally as soon as the eighth house bond inevitably raises one or both partners' psychological issues.

Uranus or Saturn in the ninth house: With Aquarius rising and Uranus here, the philosophy of life that can most help make this person's life meaningful might be "To thine own self be true" or, like the song, "I did it my way." With Aquarius rising and Saturn here, the motto can shift to "D.I.Y. (Do It Yourself),"or, as The Chofetz Chaim once said, "A lack of accomplishment is the greatest suffering."

Uranus or Saturn in the tenth house: It's hard to describe the right vocation for an Aquarian Ascendant with Uranus here because, as a poster for a book by Hunter S. Thompson says, "When the going gets weird, the weird turn pro." Levity aside, these people need to write their own unique job descriptions. With Saturn here, they need to represent integrity as well as authenticity as part of their public identity. Both types are happier being self-employed.

Uranus or Saturn in the eleventh house: With Uranus here, this person should individuate more and more with age. This is true for all of us, but particularly so in this case—this person should become a colorful, independent and quite possibly eccentric little old man or woman. With Saturn here, he or she will want to keep accomplishing Great Works *of her or her own choosing* well into old age. Both types need independent-minded associates.

Uranus or Saturn in the twelfth house: With Uranus here, the Aquarius rising person needs some altered-state time (preferably of the harmless sort) devoted to inner work. His or her inner guru is a rebel who would counsel finding one's own mystical or contemplative path rather than joining an organized religion. With Saturn here, the inner guru would recommend a more focused and methodical approach to inner work: a regularly kept dream journal, a serious meditation practice, etc.

ASCENDANT IN PISCES:

The Symbols: This person has come into the world wearing the mask of the Mystic, the Psychic, the Contemplative or the Visionary. Other images for Pisces rising include the Priest/Priestess, the Meditator, the Illusionist, or the Dreamer. Less than optimal responses to this Ascendant might include the Space Cadet, the Fragile Flower, the Addict, the Ungrounded One, or the Burnout.

The Style: This Ascendant is particularly complex to describe in modern Western terminology with its typically external orientation, so we'll spend some extra time here.

A man or woman with Pisces rising has reached an evolutionary stage where he or she must present a gentle, expansive, compassionate face to the world. Virtually essential is the development of what's usually considered a mystical sensibility: that there is a fundamental, underlying unity to all existence and a spiritual equality to all sentient beings, and that there are far more dimensions of reality than the ones we see on the evening news. Those attitudes need to ooze out through a Pisces Ascendant's pores. Those attitudes are usually easier to maintain if they're supported by a regular meditative-like process, some sort of non-damaging altered state.

Basically, this meditative process has two steps. The first step is disengaging the ego's or personality's attention from the outside world and putting it on hold, so that we can cease to identify the ego as the totality of our being. The second step is turning the attention inward, so that we can observe ourselves as *consciousness* as well as personality. If we do the first step without doing the second one, then we daydream, lose track of time, forget things, or may deliberately numb the personality in less than healthy ways. Alcohol and drugs are two possibilities for such numbing. However, any behavior that becomes addictive or compulsive—eating, sleeping, shopping, sex—and that leaves us in a trance-like, more or less numbed state *without our taking the second step of observing our consciousness,* can function as a substitute for this meditative process.

How can a Pisces rising person enter this process in a healthy way? Meditation is one method, but so are: creativity in which we can lose ourselves; prayer; contemplation; quiet time; inner work; watching sunsets; doing yoga; "runner's high;" mind-body centering techniques, etc. As I've heard a yoga teacher say, "Almost anything can function as a meditation, as long as you maintain awareness of *what part of you is performing that action* and of *what part of you is watching yourself perform that action.*" Such behavior helps a Pisces Ascendant maintain an outer style of warm, compassionate, gently humorous attunement to others.

If the rest of the chart is more linear, bold, harsh or self-contained, this Ascendant is meant to soften this person's presentation and help it be warmer and more flexible. If the rest of the chart is mild, subjective or imaginative, the Ascendant is meant to reinforce it, give it a transpersonal dimension and help it express itself. In either case, this rising sign's demeanor should convey the message: "Here is a person who gets the 'cosmic joke:' that *everyone* is a combination of soul and personality, of consciousness and ego, and that the posturings of people who don't know that yet are best approached with sympathy and humor if possible, rather than with anger and judgment."

If the childhood circumstances were rough, stronger people with Pisces rising may have an extra tendency to retreat into a well-defended fantasy world as their "altered state," until they learn that such retreats can carry dangers all their own. More fragile people may retreat into addictive behavior. They may also or alternatively reproduce the ambiance of the traumatic childhood in situations that are eerily reminiscent of it, until they recognize that Now is not Then—for Pisces rising, reality and time can be very fluid—and that they can make better choices now.

The Persona and the Other—the First House/Seventh House Axis:

Someone who *overidentifies* with a Pisces Ascendant can generally go one of two routes. The first could be described as Too Heavenly to Be of Any Earthly Good. The concept of *flight into light* comes into play here. It's possible to use religion or meditation as forms of escapism. Reality is too harsh? "I'll just meditate and stay serene; it's all an illusion anyway." Or: "Why strive to change reality when I'll get my reward in the sweet by and by?" Failure to protect oneself from predatory people can occur, if the Pisces Ascendant is so naïvely focused on a man's lovely soul that he or she ignores the switchblade in his hand. In extreme versions, while Pisces rising is being long-suffering and transcendent and ethereal, the roof is leaking, the rent's overdue and the spouse is abusing the children . . .

The second route more resembles giving up, and consists of darker ways to numb the personality. The junkie. The burnout. The victim. Milder versions include potentially quite functional people who've surrendered their own competence and sovereignty, and retreated into *learned helplessness* and various forms of fantasy. "I just don't *understand* the concepts of time and deadlines . . . " The outer lives of these people can grow well-nigh as chaotic as those who took the first route.

These examples are of course *not* the typical expressions of healthy Pisces Ascendants. They are only what may happen with *overidentification* with this Ascendant. (Please see Chapter Two for a discussion of the dynamic of overidentification.)

If this extreme expression of Pisces rising occurs, how might the seventh-house Other react? It's possible that the Other may be polarized into various Virgo responses.

The Other may say, "I can't relate to someone who doesn't know enough to come out of La-La Land. If I stay, I'll be taking care of a scatterbrained child or worse. I'm leaving."

The Other may react with Virgo criticism and try to needle the Pisces rising person into more responsible behavior. Or the Other may "serve" the Pisces Ascendant by turning into a Virgoan sort of personal assistant, reminding the Pisces rising person to eat, sleep, pay the bills on time and get the car inspected. That situation may go on for years. If and when the Other can no longer stomach handling reality for the Pisces Ascendant, he or she may look for a more grounded and fully present partner. And the Pisces rising person will feel wounded, victimized, misunderstood and harshly abandoned by that "earthbound" creature.

How might this dynamic be avoided?

If you have Pisces rising, *listen* when your partner says something like, "I think you may be too unrealistic here. Could we please consider the facts?" Or when your partner says, "You have simply got to start paying more attention and taking more responsibility. I can't shoulder everything by myself." Try to see your partner's point of view. Think a few steps ahead and consider the logical consequences of your continued absent-mindedness or escapism. You won't lose contact with your inner life thereby, and you can make your outer life run a whole lot more smoothly.

If you have Pisces rising, think carefully about what most influences your choice of partner. Of course you're drawn to Virgoan groundedness and responsibility, and fascinated with Virgo's facility with details. In an evolutionary sense, you do well to have such qualities in your mate so that your Mystic's mask can learn how to function well in the outer world as well as explore the inner one. But are you looking *only* for someone to handle life's practicalities for you? Of course you're drawn to Virgo's ability to excel at his or her craft. In an evolutionary sense, you need such qualities in a mate so that he or she can model how to anchor some of those Piscean visions in reality. But are your mate's accomplishments *all* that matter to you? You're perfectly capable of learning to focus enough to have accomplishments of your own.

The Vehicle and the Terrain: This person arrived on the planet with a vehicle (the Pisces Ascendant) that is intended to move through life as a kind of ongoing meditation (the terrain). In other words, someone with Pisces rising needs the terrain of altered-state experiences, experiences that create the possibility of acknowledging that one is more than the body and the ego, the possibility of observing one's consciousness. The experiential fuel this Pisces vehicle needs can be disorienting or visionary. The terrain it should cover is anywhere that mystical awareness can come into play—potentially everywhere, hence the Protean nature of this sign, which has been said to contain the experiences of all the other signs.

Once I heard the spiritual teacher Ram Dass tell a story that, although he doesn't have Pisces rising, serves as a good illustration for the vehicle and terrain of this Ascendant. Ram Dass was driving down the road one day chanting a mantra, getting progressively happier and feeling more and more loving, peaceful and at one with the scenery around him. Then a cop pulled him over. It didn't bother affect his mood one bit; he was one with the road, one with the sunny afternoon, one with Nature and one with the cop, whom he greeted with a big smile and a "How are you today, Officer?"

"Fine," said the cop, blinking, clearly unused to such a pleasant reception. "Uh, did you know you were doing 44 miles per hour in a 55 zone, sir? Is everything all right?"

Ram Dass, still beaming and mellow and sending out positive energy, said everything was fine; he just hadn't noticed how slowly he was driving, and apologized. He felt as if the cop were playacting at being a cop, and that the "act" was a charming cosmic joke, because he, Ram Dass, knew that the cop was really a limitless Spirit connected to the entire universe. The cop didn't give him a ticket, but he didn't get back in his cruiser either. He asked some questions about Ram Dass's car, where he was from and where he was going. Ram Dass was a bit puzzled at first, then realized the cop was enjoying the good energy so much that he just didn't want to leave. They struck up a conversation and chatted for a long time by the side of the road in the sun. Then Ram Dass drove to a bank, still feeling at one with everything and seeing everyone's Spirit. Now he felt as if the bank teller were playacting at being a teller but, he told his audience, he resisted the temptation to lean over the counter and say, "I know who you *really* are."

That's what I mean when I say the Piscean terrain can be, potentially, everywhere you go and everything you do, as long as you maintain an awareness of your inner life of Consciousness along the way.

Roadblocks arise if someone with this Ascendant numbs his or her sensitivity with some form of escapist behavior. That can happen if he or she gets stuck in the first step of meditation, putting the outer personality on hold, without taking the second step of observing the consciousness. Some of those roadblocks are fierce—too many drugs, too much alcohol, too much helplessness in the face of life's inevitable responsibilities—and may wind up damaging the personality or interfering with the person's health. A skillful use of the Pisces Ascendant involves choosing wisely how one alters one's consciousness.

If you are an atheist with Pisces rising, you don't have to believe in anything to do a good job with this Ascendant, but you still need a meditative practice, some way to turn your attention inward and observe the structure of your mind. Here's a simple way: for about fifteen or twenty minutes, sit upright, close your eyes and pay attention to your breathing. When your mind wanders, gently bring your attention back to your breathing. See if you can have some periods of time, however short, with no thoughts, just awareness of your breathing. If you maintain this practice regularly over time, you'll notice that you are calmer and more able to concentrate in all areas of your life, not just when meditating.

Staying Comfortable in the Body: Paradoxically, this process begins by not over-identifying with the body, not taking it too seriously. As Pema Chodron says, "Limit your time at the gym." Matter is energy is matter is energy, and right now the body happens to be matter, is the attitude to take here. But don't go in the other direction and think of your body as some sort of dirty cage. Your consciousness is in this physical form, and you need to maintain that form in reasonably good condition, or it will be much harder to learn what you've come here to learn. There's nothing wrong with that form—and nothing right with it, either. Treat it well, but neutrally. To paraphrase Ram Dass, you know who you really are.

Images for a Costume: A mystic's robes. A monk's or nun's robes. An Elf's ears; a faery's wings. A psychic's crystal ball. A sleepwalker's bemused expression. A mermaid's tail. A meditator's calm demeanor. A junkie's thousand-yard stare. A Rip Van Winkle suit. Virtual reality goggles. A costume from some other dimension.

Images for the Vehicle: A transporter beam. A spacecraft that can cross n-dimensional, folded space, like the ships in C.J. Cherryh's *Chanur* series. A Ford Escape. A Mercury Mariner. A magical mystery tour bus; a yellow submarine. The *Marie Celeste*; the *Flying Dutchman*. Any vehicle or vessel that carries you to another reality and/or doesn't wholly belong in this one.

Images for the Terrain: A meditation or yoga retreat. A synchronized swimming class. A film set. Backstage at a high fashion show. A special effects or holographic art studio. Anywhere an illusion is being created. An experiment in lucid dreaming. The Land of Oz. Brigadoon. Shangri-La. Anywhere a compassionate, humorous, imaginative response would come in handy. Any terrain one has to cross by intuition or in an altered state.

The Ambassador's Host Country—Neptune's and Jupiter's House Positions:

For a Pisces Ascendant, both rulers, Neptune and Jupiter, should be considered. Their house placements show the areas of life where someone with Pisces rising most needs to remember that he or she is more than just an ego, body or personality.

Neptune or Jupiter in the first house: A one-pointed expression of Pisces rising is needed here, as if this person needs to "stay in uniform." A double dose of experiences that involve letting go of defining oneself as merely personality, and learning to experience an inner reality, is needed here. That could include imaginative arts that involve creating an illusory world; social work; laughing meditations; etc. If this person overdoes the Ascendant, consciousness is altered in less than healthy ways, or the person drifts and daydreams (Neptune) or grandiosely fantasizes (Jupiter) his or her way through life.

Neptune or Jupiter in the second house. "Where your treasure is, there your heart is also," might be the motto for this placement. With Neptune here, healthy self-esteem depends on valuing one's ability to *perceive consciousness*, rather than trying to glamorize the ego. With Jupiter here, self-worth is aided by a positive, expansive, generous attitude, rather than conceit. Both placements need to be careful about acquiring "cool" or ostentatious possessions to prop up the ego from without, rather than changing the attitude from within.

Neptune or Jupiter in the third house: With Neptune here, this person needs to communicate imaginatively, even enchantingly, but also to avoid vagueness and obfuscation. Information may come from right-brained processing or even psychic awareness. Careful assessment is needed to make sure one's perceptions are realistic, however non-linear. With Jupiter here, one needs to communicate optimistically and enthusiastically, and to avoid exaggeration or aggrandizement. Any communicative process can improve this person's mood.

Neptune or Jupiter in the fourth house: Someone with Pisces rising and Neptune here needs to understand how his or her family of origin, particularly one parent, dealt with the planet of consciousness, mysticism or escapism. This person also needs his or her "hobbit hole" in which to free-float, muse and do Neptunian work. With Jupiter here, one needs to understand how one's family of origin, particularly one parent, dealt with the energies of optimism, enthusiasm and faith, or grandiosity and dogmatism. This person also needs to create a home that's a tonic and a mood-lifter.

Neptune or Jupiter in the fifth house: Neptune here indicates a need for highly imaginative, illusion-invoking creative effort that receives positive feedback, and a need to "fall in like," if not in love, with people who are expressing their own Neptunian energies in healthy ways. There's also a need for spontaneous fun. With Jupiter here, exuberant creativity is a great antidepressant, and one should "fall in like" with healthy Jupiter types: expansive, tolerant and forward-thinking rather than egotistical.

Neptune or Jupiter in the sixth house: With Neptune here, this person needs meaningful work and/or mentoring that allows the skillful use of compassion, vision and imagination. He or she should also be careful about boundaries and burnout. With Jupiter here, the Pisces rising person needs meaningful work and/or mentoring that allows the skillful use of humor, an ability to see positive outcomes, and an ability to encourage and inspire. Care should be taken not to promise more than one can deliver.

Neptune or Jupiter in the seventh house: With Neptune here, the Pisces rising person needs to bring consciousness into the sphere of marriage, friendship and partnership. Ideally, such intimates should express their sensitivity in constructive ways, rather than addictive or helpless ones. With Jupiter here, a Pisces Ascendant needs expansive intimates with a larger-than-life quality, who encourage rather than dominate or disappoint him or her.

Neptune or Jupiter in the eighth house: With Neptune here, this person needs to feel that mating involves an intermingling of souls, not just bodies. People with escapist or irresponsible tendencies should be avoided. Time should be spent exploring the shamanistic and psychological dimensions of this house, preferably from a transpersonal, mystical point of view. With Jupiter here, this person needs a sunny-natured, generous but not overbearing mate, and will experience increased faith and optimism by investigating the numinous side of the eighth house.

Neptune or Jupiter in the ninth house: With Neptune here, this person does well with a philosophy of life that embraces mysticism and exploration of consciousness, but avoids learned helplessness. Meditation may be deepened by unfamiliar settings. With Jupiter in this house, the Pisces Ascendant flourishes with a "nothing ventured, nothing gained" attitude, and finds personal renewal in evolving an optimistic world view. Especially in younger years, care should be taken to avoid grandiosity or feeling bulletproof.

Neptune or Jupiter in the tenth house: Neptune here indicates a need for a public identity representing *consciousness* to the community. Healthy representations include anyone working with the inner, creative or spiritual life: pastors, mystics, yogis, counselors, artists, etc. The lower path is that of the Bad Example: the addict, victim or otherwise dysfunctional person. With Jupiter here, this individual needs a public identity as a benevolent, philosophical, ethical, broad-minded coach or sage, rather than a dogmatic fundamentalist of any stripe.

Neptune or Jupiter in the eleventh house: With Neptune here, this person needs allies and goals that involve the exploration of consciousness. Care should be taken not to drift aimlessly into old age, and not to seek associates who want to numb consciousness rather than investigate it. With Jupiter here, a Pisces rising person needs inspiring (although not inflated) allies and goals, and to feel that the future can always hold possibilities.

Neptune or Jupiter in the twelfth house: With Neptune here, the "inner guru" has a message we might expect: meditate, and go within. Extra time spent in this process, which requires some privacy and "down time," will yield increased calm and energy. Extra time spacing out will make the outer world that much more difficult to navigate. With Jupiter here, the "inner guru" counsels open-hearted, open-handed good works, and a spiritual practice of finding the good in any situation, without resorting to gullible optimism.

PLANETS IN THE FIRST HOUSE:

Planets in the first house become part of the "wardrobe" of that Ascendant. A few comments about each planet's position in the first house are listed below. What if more than one planet is in the first house? Then that person has a lot of "costumes" in that wardrobe, at least one for each planet and one for the actual rising sign, which should take precedence in the analysis of that Ascendant.

Sun in the first house: This person should cultivate an additional costume that is *solar:* impressive, charismatic, generative and warm. Others may assign a lot of natural authority to him or her. The development of a strong will, but not a big ego, is important. Read the section on the Ascendant in Leo.

Moon in the first house: These people should develop an additional costume that is *lunar:* gentle, imaginative, receptive and reflective. They should learn to follow their hearts, honor their feelings and not fear showing them and acting on them. Failure to do so can produce moodiness until those feelings are examined. Read the section on the Ascendant in Cancer.

Mercury in the first house: This person should develop an additional costume that is Mercurial: articulate, perceptive and curious, without too much nervousness and empty chatter. They should learn to communicate as well as they possibly can. Read the section on the Ascendant in Gemini. (The Ascendant in Virgo section may also be helpful, but less relevant.)

Venus in the first house: This person should develop an additional costume that is Venusian: courteous, gracious and poised, without being either slick or a pushover. A creative outlet is a big plus. Read the section on the Ascendant in Libra. (The Ascendant in Taurus section may also be helpful, but less relevant.)

Mars in the first house: This person needs to develop an additional costume that is Martial: courageous, frank and assertive, without being pushy or belligerent. He or she should learn to have firm boundaries, and having adventures would be a good way to feed that Mars. Read the section on the Ascendant in Aries. (The Ascendant in Scorpio section may also be helpful, but less relevant.)

Jupiter in the first house: This person needs to develop an additional costume that is Jovial: larger-than-life, optimistic, tolerant and humorous, without being bombastic or presumptuous. Living according to his or her principles, without being self-righteous, can be very helpful. Read the section on the Ascendant in Sagittarius. (The Ascendant in Pisces section may also be helpful, but less relevant.)

Saturn in the first house: This person should develop an additional costume that is Saturnine: dignified, responsible, competent and reserved, without being cold or controlling. The development of self-sufficiency and practicality is important. Read the section on the Ascendant in Capricorn. (The Ascendant in Aquarius section may also be helpful, but less relevant.)

Uranus in the first house: This person should cultivate an additional costume that is Uranian: unique, free-thinking and independent, without being gratuitously weird. The more centered he or she feels, the more "different" he or she may look to others. Read the section on the Ascendant in Aquarius.

Neptune in the first house: This person should develop an additional costume that is Neptunian: visionary, compassionate and mystical, without being scattered, helpless or flaky. A regular meditative practice would be very wise. Read the section on the Ascendant in Pisces.

Pluto in the first house: This person should cultivate an additional costume that is Plutonian: psychologically sophisticated, honest and perceptive, without being sarcastic, cynical or brooding. Care should be taken not to act out one's wounded side. Read the section on the Ascendant in Scorpio.

The South Node in the first house: The Nodes of the Moon are a highly complex concept in and of themselves. The South Node represents our karmic or psychological inheritance from our past. Think of it as the past karma that most affects us in this lifetime, and that can therefore continue to show up in strong tendencies toward certain habits or situations long into adulthood. Just as we can try to create an environment with psychological parallels to our childhood, we can also try to create an environment that parallels our karmic history. For the purposes of this book, think of the South Node as *ingrained habit patterns from the past.*

But the Ascendant is how we are incarnating *now*, today. It represents the vehicle we most need to adopt in order to help our passage through *this* lifetime.

So what could the South Node in the first house mean? We can think about this placement two different ways.

If the South Node is in the first house and *conjunct*s the Ascendant within about twelve degrees, especially if it's in the same sign as the Ascendant, then this person had both a powerful will and a very well-developed persona in his or her karmic past. These people *may* have been some sort of leaders, partly because they didn't learn much about compromising and harmonizing with others—didn't learn much about the seventh house, in other words. They may have overidentified with that strong persona at the cost of the rest of the chart. Such patterns may have shown up in this lifetime's childhood as well.

If the South Node is in the first house but does *not* conjunct the Ascendant, then this person also had a strong will, may have been some sort of leader, and may not have learned much about relating. However, there's far less likelihood that he or she overdeveloped and overidentified with the persona than there is if the South Node actually conjuncts the Ascendant itself.

In either case, part of this person's evolutionary journey toward his or her seventh house North Node will involve learning to trust, to negotiate, to form "I-thou" relationships, and to throw his or her lot in with someone else rather than going it alone.

The North Node in the first house: The North Node of the Moon represents the astrological energies with which we are the *least* familiar, that which we have done and been the *least* in the karmic past. Therefore, we least understand this particular house and sign, and we probably feel and behave the most awkwardly there, not from stupidity or willfulness, but from sheer ignorance of and lack of experience with this house and sign.

If the North Node in the first house conjuncts the Ascendant within about twelve degrees, especially if it's in the same sign as the Ascendant, there's a good possibility that in the karmic past, this person had some trouble expressing his or her persona (Ascendant) in a healthy, well-integrated way, as well as some trouble developing his or her own will (first house). These people may have allowed themselves to be too influenced by their relationships (south node in the seventh house). Such patterns may have shown up in this lifetime's childhood as well. Part of this person's evolutionary journey toward the North Node will involve learning to become comfortable in the skin of his or her Ascendant in this lifetime, and to follow where that Ascendant vehicle needs him or her to go. Another part involves being less dependent on others to show him or her the way.

If the North Node is in the first house but is *not* conjunct the Ascendant, then this person's evolutionary work still revolves around developing faith in the power of his or her own will, and learning to defer less to others. However, it's *less* likely that he or she didn't have a well-functioning persona in the karmic past than is the case for someone with the North Node actually conjunct the Ascendant.

**Please visit the website of
Jodie Forrest and Steven Forrest**

www.sevenpawspress.com

**for complete information
about our products and services:**

* various types of astrological consultations
* written, computerized astrological reports
  based on your birth data
* our schedule of astrological workshops,
  intensives, lectures and other classes
* recorded lectures and DVDs
* astrology, fantasy and mythology books
* astrological software
* famous people's birthdays
* how to order a copy of your birth certificate
* and lots more material—see the site map!